SIMONE WEIL

An Apprenticeship in Attention

Mario von der Ruhr

continuum

Continuum

The Tower Building
11 York Road
London
SE1 7NX

80 Maiden Lane
Suite 704
New York
NY 10038

www.continuumbooks.com

First published 2006

British Library Cataloguing-in-Publication Data
A catalogue record for this book is available from the British Library

ISBN 0 8264 5823 8 (hardback)
ISBN 0 8264 7462 4 (paperback)

Typeset by YHT Ltd, London
Printed and bound by Ashford Colour Press Ltd., Gosport, Hants.

For my mother and Sarah

Contents

Acknowledgements

I would like to thank the Simone Weil reading group at Lampeter, especially David Cockburn, John Daniel, and Ilham Dilman, for many stimulating discussions of Weil's work, as well as Howard Mounce, D. Z. Phillips, Ieuan Lloyd, Marius Felderhof and John Kinsey for drawing my attention to aspects of Weil's thought that would otherwise have eluded me.

I am also grateful to Andrew Walby for seeing the book through the final stages of production, and indeed to Timothy Bartel for his superb work as copy-editor. My greatest debt, however, is to the Editor of this monograph series, Brian Davies, without whose infinite patience and invaluable critical comments the manuscript would not have found its way into print. Its shortcomings are, of course, entirely my own.

Lastly, I gratefully acknowledge Kunjana Thomas's permission to reprint 'The Island' and 'Absence' from R. S. Thomas's *Later Poems 1972–1982* (London: Papermac, 1984), and Orion Books' permission to quote the last stanza of 'Apostrophe', from R. S. Thomas's *Collected Poems 1945–1990* (London: Phoenix, 2004).

Mario von der Ruhr
Swansea
June 2006

Abbreviations

SN	*On Science, Necessity, and the Love of God*
SWR	*Simone Weil Reader*
SWW	*Simone Weil: Writings*
WG	*Waiting for God*

Introduction

Simone Weil was described by André Gide as 'the best spiritual writer of this century', by the existentialist philosopher Gabriel Marcel as a 'witness to the absolute', and by T. S. Eliot as 'a kind of genius akin to that possessed by the saints'. Her work impressed Albert Camus no less than Flannery O'Connor, Iris Murdoch, Julien Green, Alberto Moravia, and Thomas Merton; and even Pope John XXIII, when still a papal nuncio in Paris, was so taken with it that he wrote to tell her parents.

In spite of these accolades, however, many readers are likely to regard Weil's liberal-humanist upbringing and firm resolution to stay outside the Church, her refusal to be baptised, her sympathies for Marxist and socialist ideals, and her unorthodox attitude towards such issues as the Incarnation, the nature of the miraculous, and the hope for immortality, as poor credentials for the title of 'outstanding Christian thinker', and they are inclined to contrast her work unfavourably with that of Anselm, Augustine, and St Paul on the one hand, and Niebuhr, Bultmann, Rahner, or Barth, on the other. The purpose of this monograph is to show that the categorisation of Weil as, at best, an 'honorary' Christian is seriously mistaken, and that an introductory volume on her thought is to be welcomed for the reflection it invites on the nature of a Christian life, for what Weil has to say about Christianity at its deepest, for the light she sheds on the relation between religious belief and atheism, and for the cautiously ecumenical spirit in which she approaches not only the various manifestations of Christianity, but other religious faiths.

A further reason for welcoming the inclusion of Simone Weil in the present series is that, of the volumes published in it so far, only three – on Teresa of Avila, Catherine of Siena, and Edith Stein – are on female Christian thinkers, and that Simone Weil would make a worthy addition.

While the author's own interest in Simone Weil's work is primarily philosophical, an introductory monograph on the philosophical issues in her œuvre would be both unnecessary and unduly restrictive. Quite apart from the fact that these issues – in the philosophy of language, philosophy of religion, and philosophy of science – have been extensively discussed elsewhere (e.g. by Peter Winch, Rush Rhees, D. Z. Phillips, Eric Springsted, Richard Bell and others), such a narrow treatment would hardly do justice to the breadth of Weil's concerns, which are not merely philosophical but literary, historical, political, and religious. For this reason, the present volume is directed at general readers who have little or no previous knowledge of the subject, although the author would also expect the discussion to be helpful to academic readers with a background in philosophy, theology, history, political theory, or educational science.

Structurally, the various chapters should be seen as elaborations on the material presented in the biographical sketch (Chapter 1). Whether one thinks of Simone Weil as a teacher, manual labourer, political activist, or religious believer, thought and action are always closely interconnected for her. The purpose of the subsequent chapters is not only to make this connection more transparent, but to show how Weil's reflections throw a distinctive light on the meaning of such things as education, manual labour, political activity, and religious worship. The order in which these issues are taken up follows roughly the chronology of Weil's life and its thematic division into (a) her own education and pursuit of truth in the spirit of love (1909–32), (b) a phase of predominantly political reflection (1932–38), and (c) a phase of intense religious reflection (1938–43). In all this, Weil's rich conceptual tapestry is held together by a common thread, identified in Chapter 2 as the notion of *i'attente* (attention), with important implications for philosophical reflection, moral deliberation, political activity, and religious belief. These implications are developed in Chapters 3, 4 and 5–7, respectively, and should enable the reader to see, not only how Weil's thinking is crystallised in this central idea of attention, but why the concluding lines of Welsh poet R. S. Thomas's 'Apostrophe' could serve as a fine and poignant expression of Weil's spiritual labours:

> There are no journeys,
> I tell them. Love turns
> on its own axis, as do beauty and truth,
> and the wise are they
> who in every generation
> remain still to assess their nearness
> to it by the magnitude of their shadow.[1]

Weil's writings reveal what such stillness and spiritual self-assessment may come to. If her life nevertheless ended on a melancholy note, it was partly because she found the shadow cast by her own endeavours to be still so desperately far from Beauty and Truth, and partly because she was pained at the recognition that much of what she had to say would either not be heard at all, or else misunderstood. This introduction to her thought is intended as a small contribution to disseminating her reflections and forestalling their misinterpretation.

1

Simone Weil's Life

A. Childhood, adolescence, and university education
(1909–1932)

Simone Weil was born in Paris on 3 February, 1909, the second child of Bernard Weil and Selma Reinherz. Descended from a long line of businessmen, Bernard was the only intellectual on his side of the family tree, and soon developed a vocation to become a doctor. His attitude towards religion oscillated between agnosticism and atheism, but he was a kind, unassuming, and tolerant man, and greatly respected his own mother's deep devotion to the Jewish faith. Simone's mother Selma came from a family of Galician Jews, and was born in Russia. Her parents, too, were in the trade business, but in addition had a strongly artistic vein, with her father composing poetry in Hebrew, and her mother developing into a highly talented pianist. Unlike Bernard's parents, however, they were not practising Jews. Simone thus grew up in a family that already exhibited a broad spectrum of attitudes towards religious belief, though she herself was neither raised in the Jewish faith, nor aware of the distinction between Jews and Gentiles until she was ten years old.

The accounts we have of the Weil household reveal a highly cultured family, who had little regard for material wealth or even comfort. On the contrary, Selma ensured that her children had a Spartan upbringing, and placed much emphasis on outdoor sports activities, including hiking, cycling, rugby, dance, and gymnastics. Simone pushed herself to the limit to perform well in these, even though her physical constitution was frail, and much more prone to illness than that of her older brother André. Plagued by chronic ailments from an early age, she nevertheless bore her suffering with Stoic resilience and an astounding degree of self-effacement – dispositions that no doubt informed her intellectual precociousness and her concern for the welfare of others as well. When barely four years old, she already impressed doctors at a Parisian hospital with her wide-ranging vocabulary, and soon began to recite Cyrano de Bergerac, Corneille, Racine, even mathematical formulae, to her brother André, who also taught her to read the newspaper at six. At the age of ten, she was reading English children's books and even wrote her own fairytale, 'The Fire Sylphs', which was published posthumously in *Le Figaro Littéraire* in 1962.

Unlike other girls her age, Simone never played with dolls, could not be persuaded to take up needle and thread for sewing, and was wholly indifferent to jewellery: 'I do not like luxury', the barely three-year-old told her cousin on being presented with an expensive ring, and this attitude towards worldly goods would stay with her for the rest of her life. Far more important, in her view, was the plight of the poor and afflicted, for whose relief she was already going well beyond the call of duty: when the war broke out in 1914, for example, she made a point of giving up all her sugar and chocolate, so that these could be sent to needy soldiers on the front.

Simone's relation to her brother André, who would later become one of the leading mathematicians of his age, was one of great spiritual kinship. Completely inseparable, they formed 'a magical and informative solidarity', or, as André himself put it, 'two instruments tuned to the same note',[1] sharing with each other everything they learnt and joining in common childhood pranks, such as knocking on the doors of strangers and shouting, 'We are dying of hunger; our mama and papa are letting us die of hunger,' reaping generous donations of sweets and biscuits as a result.[2] And while they also fought with each other, a quarrel was always seen as 'a sort of magical duel of honour'[3] that would leave their friendship completely intact. Simone could not help copying her brother in everything he did, even playing soccer, but it was his preoccupation with mathematics, geometry and classical science from which she gained the most for her intellectual development.

Simone's childhood was undoubtedly a happy one, but it was also marked by a certain restlessness and instability. When the war broke out in 1914, her father was called up and, due to his frequently changing medical assignments, had to embark on an odyssey that took his family from Paris to Neufchâteau, Menton, Mayennes, Chartres, and Laval, and finally back to Paris. As a consequence, the children's education was constantly interrupted and needed to be supplemented with private tuition at home.

Jacques Cabaud notes that the young Simone was 'not a demonstrably affectionate child',[4] that she avoided physical contact and felt uncomfortable embracing or kissing even those whom she knew well. One reason for this aversion to physical contact had to do with the family's phobia toward germs and the hair-raising stories told by the bacteriologist Elie Metchnikoff, a friend of the Weils and a frequent guest at their home. On one occasion, as he kissed Simone's hand, she burst into tears and ran away, screaming for water. The history of these reactions probably began with the acute appendicitis that troubled her when she was still young. Anxious to protect her daughter from microbes, Selma Weil was adamant that her children always wash their hands and open doors with their elbows, and never kiss anyone.

Another reason for Simone's lasting shyness and reserve, especially towards men, may have been that her mother never encouraged her to accentuate her femininity in the ways that women do, but instead preferred to call Simone 'our son number two' and 'Simon', and deliberately tried to do '[her] best to encourage in Simone not the simpering graces of a little girl but the forthrightness of a boy, even if this must at times seem rude', thereby reinforcing Simone's own feeling that, given her conception of life and what it was going to demand of her, it would have been better if she *had* been born as a man.[5] This does not mean, however, that she was never drawn towards a serious love relationship. As she explained to a pupil in a letter of 1935: 'I can tell you that when, at your age, and later on too, I was tempted to try to get to know love, I decided not to – telling myself that it was better not to commit my life in a direction impossible to foresee until I was sufficiently mature to know what, in a general way, I wish from life and what I expect from it.'[6] It was only when she became clear about what she expected from life that she decided to live a life of celibacy.

From 1919 onwards, Simone at last enjoyed a more regular education at the Lycée Fénelon, a junior college for girls, where she already displayed a gift for mathematics and, even more unusually, a serious interest in politics. Indeed, as Jacques Cabaud has plausibly observed, the foundations for Simone's engagement with revolutionary politics were probably laid at this time,[7] when the ten-year-old condemned the Treaty of Versailles for being grossly unfair to the enemy.

At the age of twelve, Simone first experienced the violent and chronic headaches that were to plague her for the rest of her life. These episodes were not only painful in themselves, but made it difficult for her to eat, as chewing food only aggravated the pain and tended to induce nausea. Matters got even worse when, at fourteen, she fell into a depression so severe that she seriously considered taking her life. This adolescent crisis was fuelled by a sense of intellectual inadequacy *vis-à-vis* her brother's mathematical genius and the conviction that her mediocre abilities would never enable her to acquire more than a superficial understanding of the nature and purpose of human existence.

Fortunately, Simone not only recovered, but continued to flourish in her education. Thanks to her mother's concern for her intellectual development, she had already enjoyed a privileged upbringing and was even transferred to different sections of the same school, so that she could take advantage, for example, of Charles-Brun's Greek class, or of the Romance philologist Bédier's lectures on Plato's *Crito* and *Phaedo*.[8]

In 1924, she was admitted to the baccalaureate in Classics, at the Lycée Victor Duruy. Unsure, at first, whether to specialise in philosophy or mathematics, she eventually settled on the former, though she never lost her interest in the latter. Simone's biographers describe her as an absent-minded student, who would keep ink bottles in her pocket and walk around with ink-stained clothes. Her fellow-students apparently found her intimidating, while she, in turn, tended to withdraw into herself and talk little. One of her teachers at Duruy was the well-known philosopher René Le Senne (1882–1954), who also had special interests in psychology and character analysis, and who confirmed that she was one of the best students he had encountered throughout his career.

A year later, in 1925, Weil attained her baccalaureate in philosophy, which finally allowed her to transfer to Lycée Henri IV, in preparation for the university entrance examination. Her aim was to be admitted to the prestigious École Normale Supérieure, where only the most gifted were granted a state scholarship, in return for which they had to accept a ten-year teaching contract at one of the country's numerous *lycées*. Henri IV had only just opened its doors to women, and Weil was one of only three women in a class of 30, showing herself from the first to be an outstandingly good student – serious, original, and independent.

At Henri IV, she was predominantly tutored by the philosopher Émile Chartier (1868–1951), also known as 'Alain', or, as his students preferred to call him, 'The Man'. Alain's influence on Weil was considerable. Cabaud describes him as 'a quasi-spiritual source of inspiration',[9] and Fiori as 'the sole polarizing model of her education, the Socrates of her thought and style'.[10] Alain, who was descended from farmers in Normandy and had 'the swagger of a musketeer',[11] not only introduced Weil to the work of his own teacher, Jules Lagneau (1851–1894), a perceptive commentator on the philosophy of Kant, but impressed her with his militant political activism and uncompromising rejection of anything that threatened critical and independent thinking. Passionately concerned to cultivate his students' intellects, Alain made a point of giving them a thorough background in the history of philosophy, with special emphasis on Plato, Descartes, Spinoza, and Kant, as well as an appreciation of the great works of literature, including the works of Homer, the Greek tragedians (Aeschylus, Sophocles, Euripides), Marcus Aurelius, Voltaire, and Balzac. It was in Alain's class, too, that Weil acquired her disciplined approach to writing and learned to spend at least two hours a day committing her thoughts to paper. During her time at Henri IV she also began to take an interest in trade unionism.[12]

Impressively, Weil took her university entrance examinations along with Simone de Beauvoir and came first, both women topping a list of thirty men. She was admitted to the École Normale Supérieure in 1928. Because of her interest in politics, many of her comrades thought her both a Communist and fervently antireligious, were irritated by her appearance and monotonous voice, and generally found her awkward to be around. Meanwhile, Weil was struggling to overcome her physical frailty and joined a rugby team, but the venture proved to be a disappointment. Although she was now at the École Normale, she nevertheless continued to attend Alain's classes at Henri IV. He himself was in no doubt that Weil was a first-rate thinker, and so decided to publish her philosophical reflections in *Libres propos*, including a paper on perception (20 May 1929) and one on time (20 August 1929). Alongside her philosophical research, Weil continued to be involved in political causes, drafted anti-militarist petitions, supported the League for the Rights of Man, opposed French and other kinds of colonialism, propagated a revolutionary transformation of society through non-violent means, and found herself gravitating ever closer to Marxism, as a result of which her detractors began to speak of her as 'The Red Virgin'.

But Weil did not conform to the image of the stereotypical left-wing intellectual. Instead of merely theorising about manual labour, she came to experience working-class life at first hand, by digging potatoes or regularly helping with harvests during the holidays. Moreover, since 1927 she had also been involved in adult education classes for rail workers, set up by Alain's friend Lucien Cancouët. The aptly called Groupe d'Éducation Sociale taught French, Sociology, Political Economy, and Mathematics to a group of 25 to 30 workers, with Weil's brother André contributing the mathematics lessons. In the summer of 1931, Weil passed her final examinations and received the cherished *agrégation*. Her preference was to be posted to an industrial town in northern or central France, but her request was denied and so, in September 1931, she ended up in Le-Puy-en-Vélay, a small town in the south of France, some 300 miles from Paris.

B. Teaching and revolutionary years (1932–1938)

While in Le Puy, Weil's involvement in political activities continued unabated. In her spare time, she would regularly travel to St-Étienne for exchanges with the assistant secretary of the Loire branch of the syndicalist (trade union) movement, Albertine Thévenon, with whom she explored the question of how the unions could possibly improve the workers' plight if their understanding of it was itself deficient or incomplete. As Weil would later observe in an article written for *L'Effort*: 'It is not enough to revolt against a social order founded on oppression: one has to change it, and one can't change it without understanding it.'[13]

Moved as she was by the predicament of the poor, she also gave away a substantial portion of her income, so that workers could buy books for education classes. In addition, she began to teach at the office of the Labour Exchange, where she offered lectures on French as well as on Political Economy. While the miners of St-Étienne were 'rough' types, some of whom had served in the Foreign Legion, they were nevertheless much taken with Weil, especially after she had gone down a mine shaft with them and handled a pneumatic drill. At the Lycée, meanwhile, things went well. Weil continued to teach Philosophy and Literature, but did not follow a specific curriculum or use set textbooks, as she thought these useless. Instead, she not only recommended alternative readings, but confidently followed her own teaching method. An auditor who came to inspect her teaching was impressed with what the students had learnt, but still predicted examination failure for most. His predictions came true: of Weil's fifteen students, seven were presented for examinations, but only two passed. Intent on propagating the demanding work routine that she had come to appreciate in Alain's classes, she always made her students write a lot, and stimulated them to engage in depth with her favourite authors: Plato, Descartes, Kant, Marcus Aurelius, Balzac, Stendhal, and Marx. Her friend Gustave Thibon describes just how impressive a teacher she was:

> Her gifts as a teacher were tremendous: if she was inclined to over-estimate the possibilities of culture in all men, she knew how to place herself on the level of no matter what pupil in order to teach no matter what subject. I can imagine her carrying out the duties of an elementary school teacher just as well as those of a university professor! Whether she was teaching the rule of three to a backward village urchin or initiating me into the arcana of Platonic philosophy, she brought to the task and tried to obtain from her pupil that quality of extreme attention which, in her doctrine, is closely associated with prayer.[14]

Since her reputation as a political activist and 'troublemaker' had preceded her, Weil found herself under surveillance from the moment she arrived in Le Puy, and a police report was filed for the record. Requests for her dismissal followed soon enough, but the League of the Rights of Man took the matter up and duly defended her right to freedom of speech. However, the unemployed and the workers' leaders were lumbered with fines, and at school the parents were becoming increasingly alarmed. In spite of student petitions and union support, Weil was eventually transferred. Throughout these troubled times, she never wavered in her support for the poor, went without heat and food for many days, and gave up a considerable portion of her wages.

Before she transferred to Auxerre – in October 1932 – which she favoured for its proximity to Paris, she also travelled to Germany, primarily because she was curious about the activities of the German Communist Party *vis-à-vis* the Nazis. She decided to spend much of August in Berlin and Hamburg, and was greatly impressed by the culture of the German working class there. The Party itself, however, whose political rhetoric did not seem to her to match its action on the ground, greatly disappointed her. In the various articles that she subsequently wrote on the socio-political conditions of Germany, she made a point of expressing her solidarity with the German workers, and agreed that the harsh terms of the Treaty of Versailles, which included territorial concessions and huge reparation payments on the part of the defeated Germans, was at least partly to blame for Hitler's rise to power. Weil also felt that the victory of the Communist Party in November 1933, when it gained over 6 million votes, would not mean anything in practice, as the workers who constituted it had sunk into passivity, and the Party itself had been reduced to an inefficient bureaucratic machinery.

The Communists, Weil believed, not only had an inadequate understanding of Nazism, which simply pandered to all those who wanted political change at any cost, but had refused to support the German proletariat. She thought it telling, for instance, that the three major contending parties (Social Democrats, Communists, National Socialists) had *all* proclaimed a *socialist* revolution, and that the Social Democrats, while opposing Hitler, nonetheless declined to collaborate with the Communists.

At Auxerre, she was much liked by her students, who even helped her type material for the railway workers. Once again, though, only a small proportion of students passed the final examinations (four out of twelve), with the result that the school authorities subsequently abolished the Chair of Philosophy, and Weil was dismissed in June 1933. Her next teaching assignment, which began in October that year, was at Roanne, an industrial town with a population of 60,000, from where she still continued to travel the 65 miles to St-Étienne, both for public meetings at the Labour Exchange and to support the education of the workers. Colleagues at Roanne described her as 'a fleeting, mysterious figure immersed in some great German book, such as *Das Kapital*', and thought she must be a Communist-atheist.[15]

Weil spent the Christmas of 1933 at home with her parents in Paris and, while she was there, even managed to persuade them to put up Leon Trotsky, who had come to France for a meeting with political friends and was looking for an appropriate venue. Weil was keen to take advantage of Trotsky's visit and to talk to him, but the meeting turned out to be fruitless for both, as they disagreed on nearly everything. Trotsky left exasperated: 'Why do you put me up? Are you the Salvation Army?'[16] Not much later, a disenchanted Weil told her friend Simone Pétrement: 'I have decided to withdraw

11

from every kind of politics, except for theoretical research'.[17] She also asked the authorities for a year's unpaid leave from October 1934, ostensibly for 'personal studies', but her real intention was to gain first-hand experience of factory work.

In December 1934, she started at the Alsthom factory in Paris. Her friend Boris Souvarine, who knew an administrator at the company, helped her with the venture. Weil stayed there for four months, until April 1935, occupied with drilling, operating a power press, and turning crank handles. The experience was rough. Not only did she have to put up with bullying, harassment, and injustices of various kinds, but with splitting headaches, toothache, and eczema. The work left her utterly exhausted and demoralised. She also found that women suffered more than men, as they were the first to get fired, and therefore had to be more competitive as well. There were no resting places or chairs anywhere. The threat of personal humiliation was both real and constant, and she was finding it increasingly harder to think. From April until May 1934, Weil also worked as a packer in Boulogne-Billancourt, then at the Renault factory in Paris from June till August 1934, experiencing the same drudgery as before. She soon realised that, far from prompting the workers to revolt, continuous oppression rather had the opposite effect and tended to induce apathy and passive submission. Soon after this ordeal, she left with her parents for Portugal, where she had the first of three important encounters with Catholicism:

> I entered the little Portuguese village, which, alas, was very wretched too, on the very day of the festival of its patron saint. I was alone. It was the evening and there was a full moon over the sea. The wives of the fishermen were, in procession, making a tour of all the ships, carrying candles and singing what must certainly be very ancient hymns of a heart-rending sadness. ... There the conviction was suddenly borne in upon me that Christianity is pre-eminently the religion of slaves, that slaves cannot help belonging to it, and I among others.[18]

Weil's next teaching assignment was in Bourges. In spite of her reclusiveness, the students liked her, calling her 'la petite Weil', though some of them also provoked her with articles which they knew would upset her. She joined the young factory managers' association for their regular meetings, worked on a farm, and 'in the fields ... never stopped talking about the future martyrdom of Jews, poverty, deportations'.[19] At the Rosières Foundries, she embarked on an experiment with a factory journal, *Entre nous*, which was to be produced entirely by the workers themselves. One of her own papers, on Antigone, was also published in it.

After the outbreak of the Spanish Civil War, in the autumn of 1936, Weil spontaneously decided that, her pacifist convictions notwithstanding, she had to go to Spain and support the Republicans in their fight against General Franco and his fascist supporters. She took the train for Barcelona and prudently travelled incognito as a journalist, the requisite certificate having been issued by a trade union in Paris. In Aragon, Weil joined the anarchist-syndicalist movement, but soon afterwards had an accident involving hot oil, which caused serious burns to the lower part of her leg and ankle and made hospital treatment unavoidable. Unfit for further action in Spain, she reluctantly returned to Bourges in September 1936, proudly wearing her army cap and red scarf, and wondering whether one could, perhaps, steal cannons from the local arsenal and dispatch them to Republican rebels in Spain. Unfortunately, the Spanish venture had left her health in a precarious condition, and forced her to take sick leave during the first part of the 1937/38 session. By April 1937, she was sufficiently restored for a holiday in Italy, and so decided to travel to Milan, Florence, Rome, and Assisi. Michelangelo's paintings and Leonardo's *Last Supper*, in particular, made a deep impression on her, but it was in Assisi that she finally fell on her knees:

> In 1937 I had two marvellous days at Assisi. There, alone in the little twelfth-century Romanesque chapel of Santa Maria degli Angeli, an incomparable marvel of purity where Saint Francis often used to pray, something stronger than I compelled me for the first time in my life to go down on my knees.[20]

In October of the same year, she was appointed Professor of Philosophy at the Lycée of St-Quentin, an industrial town close to Paris.

C. Religious phase (1938–1943)

Weil's third important encounter with Catholicism occurred during Easter 1938, when she visited the Abbey of Solesmes. She had heard that the Gregorian chant in the Abbey's church was particularly beautiful, and very much wanted to listen to it. In spite of excruciating headaches, and much to the amazement of the local parishioners, she attended all the services from Palm Sunday to Easter Tuesday, and was overwhelmed by the beauty of the chants.

A young Englishman, John Vernon, introduced her to the so-called 'metaphysical' poets, including George Herbert, whose poem 'Love (III)' she learnt by heart and kept reciting to herself. 'It was during one of these recitations', Weil tells us in her *Spiritual Autobiography*, 'that ... Christ himself came down and took possession of me'.[21] The experience, which occurred towards the end of 1938, was intense and deeply personal, something in which the feeling of Christ's presence combined with a deep appreciation of the Passion and the reality of divine love, even in times of affliction. But profound though the experience was, Weil hardly ever talked about it, even to her closest friends. It was too ineffable and personal to be expressed in words, let alone turned into an object of disinterested study.

A few months later, in March 1939, German troops entered Prague. Weil felt that she could no longer maintain her pacifist attitude, and so decided to abandon it, subsequently reproaching herself for not having done so sooner:

Ever since the day when I decided, after a very painful inner struggle, that in spite of my pacifist inclinations it had become an overriding obligation in my eyes to work for Hitler's destruction, with or without any chance of success, ever since that day my resolve has not altered; and that day was the one on which Hitler entered Prague – in May 1939, if I remember right. My decision was tardy, perhaps; I left it too late, perhaps, before adopting that position. Indeed, I think so and I bitterly reproach myself for it.[22]

In the summer of 1939, she applied for sick leave and once again travelled to Italy, to study some of her favourite paintings by Da Vinci, Giotto, Masaccio, Giorgione, Rembrandt, Goya, and Velázquez. After this Italian journey, Weil never taught again. But she continued to read avidly, especially Aeschylus and Sophocles, the ancient historians (Herodotus, Thucydides, Plutarch, Caesar, Tacitus), and works on the Middle Ages. In addition, she read through the entire Old Testament for the first time in her life. In the spring of 1940, she also took up the *Bhagavad Gita* and began to learn Sanskrit, so as to follow the text in the original.

On 13 June, 1940, the day before the German troops occupied Paris, Weil and her parents decided to escape to southern France, first to Vichy, and two months later to Marseilles, which had become the main gateway for those who wanted to leave the country. Once in Marseilles, Weil asked to be given a teaching post in North Africa, but her request was denied. Incessantly concerned about the plight of refugees, she visited a Vietnamese refugee camp, handed over her food coupons to the needy, and urged Marshal Pétain, whose collaborationist government was in charge of the unoccupied zone, to abolish internment as a way of punishing foreigners who were in violation of residency regulations, and indeed to pardon all those who had already been interned on such grounds.

In October 1940, the Vichy government released an anti-Jewish statute, which prohibited Jews from occupying leading positions in the army, the media, and the civil service, including education. Weil at once wrote to complain to the Minister of Education, M. Carcopino, urging him also to explain what, exactly, the term 'Jew' signified. Her letter finishes with the words: 'If nonetheless the law demands that I regard the term "Jew", whose meaning I do not know, as an epithet applicable to my person, I am disposed to submit to it as to any other law.'[23] She never received a response.

While in Marseilles, Weil also joined the Resistance movement and played an important role in the dissemination of its influential underground newspaper, *Cahiers de témoignage chrétien*. At the same time, she tried to get ration cards for German refugees by inducing her father to sign false medical certificates and, on one occasion, was summoned by the police over an intercepted draft proposal for front-line nurses, which was her audacious plan for 'a very mobile organisation' that 'should in principle be always at the points of greatest danger, to give first aid during battles'.[24] Unfortunately, her proposal for such a grand humanitarian gesture in the face of the enemy's brutality and injustice was never taken up.

From October 1940, Weil also began to write for *Cahiers du sud*, sometimes under a pseudonym ('Émile Novis', an anagram of her name), her finest contribution being the essay '*The Iliad* or The Poem of Force'. In June 1941, she encountered Father Joseph-Marie Perrin, a nearly blind Dominican priest, who had been introduced to her by her Catholic friend Helène Honnorat. Perrin, known for his generous spirit and selfless devotion to the plight of Jewish and other refugees, soon became Weil's friend and an invaluable interlocutor in their frequent philosophical and theological discussions of Christian doctrine. In one of her last letters to him, she insisted that she owed him 'the greatest debt of gratitude that I could ever have incurred toward any human being',[25] not only for his intellectual honesty and integrity, but for what their conversations had taught her about the character of her own spiritual condition.

Since Weil very much wanted to work as an agricultural labourer, Perrin readily referred her to Gustave Thibon of St-Marcel-d'Ardèche, a farmer and self-educated Catholic, who also turned out to be a staunch conservative and supporter of Pétain. Highly sceptical of left-wing Jewish intellectuals, he was doubtful at first whether he and Weil would even get along. However, he soon realized that his new visitor was not only an extraordinarily gifted teacher, but a mature and serious individual, with strong leanings towards – and many unanswered questions about – the Catholic faith. Weil subsequently agreed to work on his vineyard, where she would spend up to eight hours a day picking grapes, even in the rain. And while she knew Thibon only for a relatively short period of time, she came to regard him as a close and cherished friend. During their last encounter, in April 1942, she handed him her *Cahiers*, selections from which he published under the title *La Pesanteur et la grâce* (Gravity and Grace) a few years after her death, in 1947. To Father Perrin, Weil entrusted her *Spiritual Autobiography*, and then set off with her parents, first to Casablanca, then on to New York. She was anxious to get to London, to join the Resistance there.

Not long after her arrival in New York, in July 1942, she wrote a desperate letter to Maurice Schumann (1911–1998), a radio spokesman for Charles de Gaulle (1890–1970) and the Resistance movement during the war, in the hope that he might help her find some 'really useful work, not requiring technical expertise but involving a high degree of hardship and danger'.[26] The reason for her request was that

the suffering all over the world obsesses and overwhelms me to the point of annihilating my faculties and the only way I can revive them and release myself from the obsession is by getting for myself a large share of danger and hardship. That is a necessary condition before I can exert my capacity for work. I beseech you to get for me, if you can, the amount of hardship and danger which can save me from being wasted by sterile chagrin. In my present situation I cannot live. It very nearly makes me despair.[27]

In the meantime, she decided to take a nursing course in Harlem, to frequent the New York Public Library for detailed studies of the spiritual affinities between Western European folklore and Eastern mythology, and to attend daily mass at the nearby Catholic church, as well as Baptist services at weekends. Concurrently with these devotional exercises, she also sought to become clear about the Church's attitude towards various aspects of her own religious convictions, including the issue of baptism, and soon embarked on an extended pilgrimage to various priests and theologians who might be able to help her. The results of her quest were, however, far more sobering than she expected:

> I have seen the Jesuit to whom the nun from the convent in Brooklyn sent me. After an hour of theological discussion, he explained to me that to his great regret he travelled too often to be able to have repeated meetings with me, and that another Jesuit there, whom he named, would deal with me. That reminded me of 'It's noon, time to go to lunch'. I wonder whether this other fellow will pass me on to a third, and so on, until I'm worn out. I feel sorry for them. . . . I have become aware that even in the minds of priests, Catholicism doesn't have fixed frontiers. It is at once rigid and imprecise. There are things of 'strict faith', but it is impossible to know which they are. If one questions several priests educated in theology as to whether such and such a proposition is 'of strict faith', some say 'yes', others 'I think so', and still others 'I'd say no'.[28]

In November 1942, she could at last depart for England, having secured a post as assistant to André Philip, a commissioner of the Comité national de la France libre. Her work in London involved the analysis of committee reports from the Free Zone, and drawing up proposals for the details of a French constitution, as well as for the legal, educational, and administrative organisation of France in the post-war period. Weil's suggestions were later published in *The Need for Roots*, whose central themes are the importance of rootedness and the fulfilment of the spiritual needs (equality, hierarchy, obedience, liberty, order, truth, punishment, etc.) by which it is constituted.

Weil's health had never been particularly robust and, within a few months of her arrival in England, it began to decline rapidly. In April 1943, she had to be admitted to Middlesex Hospital, where the doctors diagnosed her with pulmonary tuberculosis and decided that it would be best to transfer her to Ashford Sanatorium in Kent. Mindful of the fact that her fellow-countrymen had to live on minimal food rations, Weil, already drained by her previous ordeals and activities in France, insisted on the same for herself, and in the process weakened herself even more. Critical though her condition was, she did not want her parents to know, and insisted that arrangements be made for her letters to be dispatched from her previous address in London. In the last of these, written just over a week before her death, she tells them that there is 'very little time or inspiration for letters now. They will be short, erratic, and far between. But you have another source of consolation. By the time you get this (unless it arrives quickly) perhaps you will also have the awaited cable. (But nothing is certain! ...) Au revoir, darlings. Heaps and heaps of love. – Simone'.[29] By the end of the following week, Simone Weil's heart and muscles had become so weak that there was no prospect of recovery. She died on 24 August 1943. The coroner's inquest, held three days later, resulted in a verdict of suicide. Even the local newspapers carried headlines about the strange case of a 'French Professor' who had 'starved herself to death'. Simone Weil was buried in Ashford Cemetery.

2

An Apprenticeship in Attention

A. Prelude

In 1948, the French publishers La Colombe released a collection of letters and essays, all of which Weil had given or sent to Father Perrin during her time in Marseilles, between 1940 and 1942. The volume was entitled *Attente de Dieu* (*Waiting on God*) and is still one of the most widely known and most readily available of her works in print, both in continental Europe and on the Anglo-American markets, where an English translation was first published in 1951. It is also an excellent introduction to some of Weil's central spiritual concerns and an insightful, retrospective illumination of her engagement with the Christian faith.

Waiting on God contains, among other things, some highly provocative remarks on school education and its relation to religious worship; a 'spiritual autobiography' charting Weil's religious development; an explanation of her hesitations concerning baptism; reflections on the love of God and the meaning of suffering; and thoughts on the Lord's Prayer.[1] Weil's reflections on these issues not only betray a passionate struggle for clarity, but a keen awareness of her own life as an ongoing apprenticeship in a certain kind of attention, without which a proper understanding of man's existential predicament is impossible.

It is fitting, therefore, that the first essay reprinted in *Waiting on God* is concerned with the notion of attention, and with the way in which a certain attitude towards learning may pave the way for a properly attentive relation to our neighbour, the natural world, and God. Indeed, Weil firmly believed that serious attention to a problem in geometry, to one's neighbour and his needs, and to God's will in prayer were all manifestations of one and the same existential calling, with far-reaching pedagogical, ethical, socio-political, religious, and theological ramifications. This is why the notion of attention may rightly be said to be a kind of Ariadne's thread running through Weil's entire œuvre, or a prism in which the various beams of her thinking are illuminatingly refracted. Consonant with the importance Weil attached to the study of literature, in the final section of this chapter I shall illustrate the difference between attention and inattention by contrasting a literary character in Thomas Mann's *The Magic Mountain* with the historical figure of Adolf Eichmann, the Nazi war criminal. Indeed, given the fragmentary nature of Weil's thoughts on attention and school education, the most fruitful approach to it seems to me an exegesis that is both interdisciplinary and open-textured, in the sense that philosophical, literary, biographical, and pedagogical observations are employed to throw further light on the various quotations from her œuvre.

B. The pursuit of truth

As with any of Weil's reflections, her thoughts on the notion of attention are grounded in personal experiences whose spiritual significance is appreciated most fully in retrospective reflection. One of these experiences, dating back to her adolescent years, is described in a letter to Father Perrin:

> At fourteen I fell into one of those fits of bottomless despair that come with adolescence, and I seriously thought of dying because of the mediocrity of my natural faculties. The exceptional gifts of my brother, who had a childhood and youth comparable to those of Pascal, brought my own inferiority home to me. ... What did grieve me was the idea of being excluded from that transcendent kingdom to which only the truly great have access and wherein truth abides. I preferred to die rather than live without that truth. After months of inward darkness, I suddenly had the everlasting conviction that any human being, even though practically devoid of natural faculties, can penetrate to

the kingdom and truth reserved for genius, if only he longs for truth and perpetually concentrates all his *attention* on its attainment.[2]

Though Weil was by no means ungifted – on the contrary, at school she soon advanced beyond her comrades and quickly gained a reputation for 'overheating' the class[3] – she was worried that intellectual progress and the attainment of a certain degree of spiritual depth might be a function of natural ability, so that access to 'that transcendent kingdom ... wherein truth abides' was strictly reserved for extraordinarily gifted individuals like her brother. If this was indeed so, then her own quest for truth must rest on an illusion. In this respect, Weil's predicament resembled that of Heinrich von Kleist (1777–1811), the German novelist and play-wright, whose every pursuit revolved around the passionate quest for an ever-higher level of learning and understanding, and who was led to the brink of suicide when, in 1801, this ideal was shattered to the core. Kleist was 24 and a student at the University of Berlin when he came across the philosophy of Immanuel Kant and con-cluded from it that 'we cannot determine whether what we call "truth" actually is the truth, or merely appears to be the truth',[4] since all experience is moulded by the nature of human cognition and thus necessarily cut off from the way things really are. Or so Kleist thought. His (mis)interpretation of Kant to the contrary notwithstanding, the realisation that he might be chasing shadows was a painful one: 'Confused by the tenets of a sad philosophy, I was unable to keep busy, unable to get anything going, unable to commit myself to a job.'[5] Kleist stopped reading and working, first contemplated suicide but then sought relief in extended travels across Europe, which helped him recover from this crisis and led him to embrace writing as his future vocation. Tragically, Kleist's literary career only lasted until 1811, when he shot himself as part of a double suicide pact with his lover Henriette Vogel.

Weil and Kleist's despair over the pursuit of truth would hardly be intelligible if 'truth' was understood in a purely intellectual or speculative sense, as a collection of otherwise indifferent 'facts' in this or that area of academic enquiry, or as a set of theoretical propositions in an architectonic philosophical system. How could a lay mathematician's inability to penetrate into the deeper regions of higher algebra or astrophysics, say, or a sceptical philosophical argument about human cognition, be sufficient to prompt despair, let alone thoughts of suicide?[6] For Weil and Kleist, however, the task was not simply that of expanding their expertise in subjects like mathematics or geometry, which they both studied with equal fervour, but clarity about *existential* concerns, including the issue of how we ought to live, and of our relation to the world in which we find ourselves. As Kleist put it:

> I would so much like to progress in a *purely humanistic* education, but knowledge makes us neither better nor happier. If only we could understand how everything hangs together! ... Am I supposed to use all these abilities and this whole life merely for getting to know another species of insect, or for according a plant its proper place in the general taxonomy of things?[7]

Kleist wanted to know what to *do*, what orientation to give his life, and at one point stubbornly refused to leave his room until he had found an answer to this question. The magnitude of the problem, which none of his academic training could help him solve, transpired when he had to confess to his sister that 'eight days went by and I eventually had to leave my room without having reached a decision. – You don't know, Ulrike, how my innermost self has been shaken to the core.'[8] Kleist's recognition that 'truth' is not reducible to the objects of scholarly expertise is echoed in Weil's remark that 'we would not search for the truth at all if it were something that did not concern us ... Truth is a means of purification. [It] is the light of the sun'.[9]

Broadly speaking, the pursuit of truth is fuelled by a passionate desire to understand how things really are, so that one's actions, too, appear under descriptions of the true and genuine, rather than under the aspect of the false and counterfeit. For this reason, and much though she disliked Nietzsche's style of thinking – she thought him arrogant and repugnant, even where she agreed with him[10] – Weil would have applauded the uncompromising spirit in which the young Nietzsche asked:

> Do we after all seek rest, peace, and pleasure in our inquiries? No, only truth – even if it be most abhorrent and ugly. ... Here the ways of men part: if you wish to strive for peace of soul and pleasure, then believe; if you wish to be a devotee of truth, then inquire.[11]

Nietzsche's devotees of truth are a far cry from the 'walking encyclopedias' or 'incarnate compendia'[12] produced by the educational institutions of his own time:

Men are to be trained for the purposes of the age to lend a hand as soon as possible: they are to labour in the factory of common utility before they are ripe, or rather to prevent their ever becoming ripe – because that would be a luxury which would withdraw a lot of strength from 'the labour market'.[13]

On this negative point, Weil is entirely at one with Nietzsche, even though her own, positive conception of the value of school education revolves around a Christian, rather than a secular, ideal of pedagogy. A more recent, and no less illuminating, expression of Weil's – and Kleist's – insights into the existential dimensions of the quest for truth comes from Wittgenstein's *Tractatus Logico-Philosophicus*, first published two years before Weil despaired over her 'mediocrity'. In this work, Wittgenstein notes: 'We feel that even when *all possible* scientific questions have been answered, the problems of life remain completely untouched.'[14]

As Kleist's case illustrates, life's deepest problems are often intertwined with questions about man's relation to the world, and thus also with the issue of whether the scientific conception of reality can make any contribution to the clarification of that relation. Initially, Kleist thought that it did, but then found that even his love of the sciences, which had frequently sustained him in times of adversity, was gradually beginning to wane.[15] His disenchantment had to do with the recognition that, valuable though an understanding of the *physical* world was, it did not give him understanding in his *life*. Weil not only shared this concern but, in addition, came to appreciate that insight into the problems of life, while not a function of one's natural abilities, nevertheless requires a certain kind of effort, a continuous apprenticeship in attention, one of whose most essential demands is an uncompromising intellectual honesty:

I have an extremely severe standard for intellectual honesty, so severe that I never met anyone who did not seem to fall short of it in more than one respect; and I am always afraid of failing in it myself.[16]

The thought that true attention is a mark of intellectual honesty, and thus a moral requirement which is not conditioned by motives of self-interest, also informs Weil's recollection that, in spite of the headaches from which she had been suffering all her life, and which were making sustained intellectual activity increasingly more

23

difficult, she was able 'to persevere for ten years in an effort of concentrated *attention* that was practically unsupported by any hope of results'.[17] The value of such extreme efforts at attention, in other words, already lies in the effort itself, irrespective of whether it yields any immediate results. Indeed, just as happiness is more easily found when it is not actively sought, so serious attention is more likely to yield results when these are not expected: 'We do not obtain the most precious gifts by going in search of them but by waiting for them'.[18]

Thus, attention as Weil understands it is also characterised by a certain sort of patience. Moreover, as she was to discover in 1938, a serious effort at attention can also reveal something about divine love, even in times of great affliction:

> I spent ten days at Solesmes, from Palm Sunday to Easter Tuesday, following all the liturgical services. I was suffering from splitting headaches; each sound hurt me like a blow; by an extreme effort of *concentration* I was able to rise above this wretched flesh, to leave it to suffer by itself, heaped up in a corner, and to find a pure and perfect joy in the unimaginable beauty of the chanting and the words.[19]

Several years later, towards the end of her life, as Weil was working in the vineyards of Gustave Thibon, she learnt to recite the Lord's Prayer in the original Greek and found that in prayer, too, an extreme effort at attention was needed for the divine word to take root, nourish, and transform:

> I recited the Our Father in Greek every day before work, and I repeated it very often in the vineyard. Since that time I have made a practice of saying it through once each morning with absolute *attention*. If during the recitation my attention wanders or goes to sleep, in the minutest degree, I begin again until I have once succeeded in going through it with absolutely pure *attention*.[20]

All of these pivotal experiences are recalled in Weil's *Spiritual Autobiography*, recorded just over a year before her death. Spanning a period of eighteen years, they not only testify to her own, extraordinary efforts at overcoming powerful obstacles – physical, psychological, and intellectual – to gain a deepened understanding of life, but reveal an intimate connection between the fruits of her school studies on the one hand, and her eventual communion with God, on the other. Hence the title of her essay: 'Reflections on the Right Use of School Studies with a View to the Love of God', which unfolds that connection in greater detail.

C. Attention and school studies

This essay was written for Father Perrin, whom Weil knew to have relations with the so-called Jécistes, a group of Christian students, in Montpellier. While it is concerned with a *Christian* conception of learning, and informed by 'the realisation that prayer consists of attention',[21] Weil insists that the spiritual effects of properly conducted school studies are quite independent of any particular religious belief.[22] This is because the cultivation of a certain kind of attention and the acquisition of spiritual depth are, in fact, internally related:

> Never in any case whatever is a genuine effort of the attention wasted. ... Perhaps he who made the unsuccessful effort will one day be able to grasp the beauty of a line of Racine more vividly on account of it. But it is certain that this effort will bear its fruit in prayer. There is no doubt whatever about that.[23]

What, then, is involved in 'a genuine effort of the attention'? Contrary to what one might expect, *attente* is not contrasted with the sort of absent-mindedness which prompts one to say 'Pay attention!' or 'Listen up!' to someone who is easily distracted by goings-on in the environment, or lost in daydreaming. For such attention would merely be 'a kind of muscular effort', which may well result in good marks and success at examinations, but otherwise has no pedagogical value whatever.[24] In order to gain genuine and deep insight into a given subject matter, it is not enough simply to register what one hears or reads. In addition, one must make it one's own, and appropriate it in ways that go deep, and what is required for this is precisely the kind of attention that is unconditioned by extraneous motives, such as the desire to impress, to advance one's career, or simply to feel good:

> If there is a real desire, if the thing desired is really light, the desire for light produces it. There is a real desire when there is an effort of attention. It is really light that is desired if all other incentives are absent.[25]

25

In spite of its undeniable spiritual effects, any genuine effort of attention is essentially an end in itself, though it may also be a necessary prerequisite for what can, in the final analysis, only be bestowed as an act of grace:

> Every time that a human being succeeds in making an effort of attention with the sole idea of increasing his grasp of truth, he acquires a greater aptitude for grasping it, even if his effort produces no visible fruit.[26]

Weil is not suggesting that a student preoccupied with a particular problem in geometry or mathematics, say, should regard its solution as unimportant, but rather that she should not try to force a solution through a sheer effort of will: 'Attention consists in suspending our thought, leaving it detached, empty, and ready to be penetrated by the object.'[27] Given that the primary purpose of school studies is to 'aim solely at increasing the power of attention with a view to prayer',[28] it follows, not only that all other considerations are of secondary importance, but that, on the contrary, these may actually get in the way of the very task at hand:

> Students must therefore work without any wish to gain good marks, to pass examinations, to win school successes; without any reference to their natural abilities and tastes; applying themselves equally to all their tasks, with the idea that each one will help to form in them the habit of that attention which is the substance of prayer.[29]

The educational desiderata expressed in this remark are, of course, radically at odds with common practice at most of the educational institutions with which we are familiar today. Here, 'natural' ability, individual intellectual taste, competitive examinations, and the prospect of economic rewards for high marks are accorded an importance which, for Weil, caricatures the very ideals that ostensibly underlie even a secular humanist education. In this connection, it is ironic that the attitude towards learning which Weil would applaud in students is far more likely to be encountered at institutions whose pedagogical approach the representatives of the educational establishment tend to deride as 'soft', or as implying a 'dumbing down' of academic standards, such as the anthroposophically oriented Steiner schools, the child-centred experimental schools propagated by Maria Montessori, or schools whose principles are informed by the alternative pedagogy of educational theorists like Ivan Illich, Jonathan Kozol, Robert Coles, or Paolo Freire.[30] As Richard Bell notes in this context:

> Freire's ideas, along with those of Ivan Illich, Jonathan Kozol, and Robert Coles, constitute a body of pedagogical literature reflecting similar moral and political concerns and projecting a set of educational ideals that are a contemporary reflection of the fragmentary ideas on education to be found in Simone Weil.[31]

Fragmentary though Weil's reflections on education are, they point up an urgent need to re-examine current pedagogical practice, as that practice may well turn out to be a travesty of any serious attempt to cultivate the only kind of attention worth possessing. As Bell rightly observes, these reflections also invite further thought on the relation between Weil's educational ideals and those of some of the leading modern educational reformers. On the other hand, it must be remembered that, whatever parallels there may be in this connection, Weil's conception of education is ultimately *theocentric*, and thus not only irreducible to pragmatist construals of pedagogy, but radically at odds with educational programmes dictated by a particular political ideology. For Weil, the end of all human action is the supernatural goal of the Christian faith, and the sole purpose of education, therefore, is to cultivate the kind of attention needed for man's journey toward that goal. As Pius XI puts it in his encyclical *Christian Education of Youth* (1929):

> The church's whole educational aim is to restore the sons of Adam to their high position as children of God. [It insists that] education must prepare man for what he should do here below in order to attain the sublime end for which he was created ... The true Christian does not renounce the activities of this life, he does not stunt his natural faculties; but he develops and perfects them, by coordinating them with the supernatural. He thus enables what is merely natural in life and secures for it new strength in the material and temporal order, no less than in the spiritual and eternal.[32]

The obstacles to a Christian education, however, are not merely *external*, such as incentives and constraints suggested by dubious educational paradigms. There are *internal* obstacles to spiritual progress, too, and it is these that lead Weil to the second of the two major conditions for putting school studies to proper use:

> To take great pains to examine squarely and to contemplate attentively and slowly each school task in which we have failed, seeing how unpleasing and second rate it is, without seeking any excuse or overlooking any mistake or any of our tutor's corrections, trying to get down to the origin of each fault. There is a great temptation to do the opposite, to give a sideways glance at the corrected exercise if it is bad and to hide it forthwith. Most of us do this nearly always. We have to withstand this temptation.[33]

Once again, the reason why this temptation is to be withstood is not so much that it slows down the learning process, though this is also true, but that it panders to something in the self which rests content with superficiality and thereby reinforces a strong inclination to inattention: 'Something in our soul has a far more violent repugnance for true attention than the flesh has for bodily fatigue.'[34] The repugnance Weil has in mind here is the ego's reluctance to engage in scrupulous self-criticism, since such criticism has a tendency to humiliate, to shatter the ego's pride and vanity. Since humility is a prime Christian virtue, there is a sense in which every act of true attention, insofar as it inspires such humility, also contributes to the purification of the soul, ridding it of some evil: 'Every time that we really concentrate our attention we destroy the evil in ourselves. If we concentrate with this intention, a quarter of an hour of attention is better than a great many good works.'[35]

What is required of me, Weil says elsewhere, is 'that attention which is so full that the "I" disappears', an effort to direct my attention completely away from myself, my wishes, preconceptions, and inclinations, and onto the object of my enquiry.[36] Thus, true attention – whether to a particular problem in geometry, to the beauty of nature, to an interlocutor in conversation, or to God in prayer – always involves an element of self-denial and thus a negative dimension, the positive one being *patience*. As Wittgenstein once said about philosophical confusion, the obstacles to be overcome in dispelling it invariably have to do with the *will* – the self's desire to cling to a particular thought, idea, or way of looking at things, simply because it is its own product – and honest reflection, therefore, requires nothing less than unremitting labour on oneself.[37] Weil says:

All wrong translations, all absurdities in geometry problems, all clumsiness of style, and all faulty connection of ideas in compositions and essays, all such things are due to the fact that thought has seized upon some idea too hastily, and being thus prematurely blocked, is not open to the truth.[38]

Attention, then, involves a kind of patience, but also, as we have seen, detachment, self-denial, and humility. It acts as a counter-weight to the self and its egocentric concerns, and instead focuses the soul on an object of enquiry in the spirit of love: 'Taken to its highest degree, [attention] is the same thing as prayer. It pre-supposes faith and love.'[39] Weil is aware of the limited degree to which school studies can cultivate this attention at present. Such studies 'only develop a lower kind of attention',[40] which, if it is to grow, especially in the direction of divine worship, also needs to engage with life outside the classroom.

Even so, school studies conducted in the right spirit can serve as an indispensable prophylactic against the very vices of thought – and, by implication, character – which get in the way of attaining that higher form of attention which 'is the very substance of prayer'.[41] Far from being the opposite of absent-mindedness, then, true attention contrasts with attachment, illusion, prejudice, the projection of personal desire, false fascination, obtuseness, pride, and vanity. The educator's most important mission, therefore, is not only the cultivation of the intellect, but the formation of character, and it is from the latter that the notion of attention derives its ethical significance. Nor could it be otherwise. For someone who, like Weil, sees the eschatological end of all human activity in God, this pedagogical ideal is the direct consequence of the exhortation to love one's neighbour. It is because such love involves a certain kind of attention that school studies have the importance they do. In this context, Weil says:

The useless efforts made by the Curé d'Ars, for long and painful years, in his attempt to learn Latin bore fruit in the marvellous discernment that enabled him to see the very soul of his penitents behind their words and even their silences.[42]

In the light of the contribution which the Curé's struggles with Latin made to the 'marvellous discernment' which informed his relations with the suffering, Weil can also say:

School children and students who love God should never say: 'For my part I like mathematics'; 'I like French'; 'I like Greek'. They should learn to like all these subjects, because all of them develop that faculty of attention which, directed toward God, is the very substance of prayer.[43]

Having sketched out the general features of Weil's distinction between attention and inattention, it may be helpful to illustrate its ethical dimension by reference to a contrast between two characters, one fictional and one historical.

D. Attention, inattention, and our neighbour

In *The Magic Mountain*, Thomas Mann sets himself the formidable task of describing the intellectual, spiritual, and moral development of his hero Hans Castorp, over a period of seven years spent at the Berghof, a sanatorium in an isolated region of the Swiss Alps. In doing so, Mann faces the problem of giving an account of Castorp's deepening understanding of important dimensions of human life (birth, death, sexuality, one's relation to one's neighbour, etc.) in a way that will also edify, and not merely entertain, the reader, in the tradition of Goethe's *Wilhelm Meister's Apprenticeship* and Gottfried Keller's *Green Henry*. If Mann succeeds in his endeavour, it is because of the way in which important experiences in Castorp's life are carefully woven into a complex network of events with which they are illuminatingly contrasted, in a way which brings out *what* Castorp can be said to have understood about his life that he had not understood before. One such crucial experience occurs in a chapter appropriately entitled 'Sudden Enlightenment', in which Hofrat Behrens, the director of the Berghof and senior physician, allows Castorp to look at a familiar part of his body, viz. his hand, through an X-ray screen. *What* Castorp sees is described by Mann as follows:

[Hofrat Behrens] was so kind as to permit the patient, at his request, to look at his own hand through the screen. And Hans Castorp saw, precisely, precisely what he must have expected, but what it is hardly permitted man to see, and what he had never thought would be vouchsafed him to see: he looked into his own grave. The process of decay was forestalled by the powers of the light-ray, the flesh in which he walked

30

disintegrated, annihilated, dissolved in vacant mist, and there within it was the finely turned skeleton of his own hand, the seal ring he had inherited from his grandfather hanging loose and black on the joint of his ring-finger – a hard, material object, with which man adorns the body that is fated to melt away beneath it, when it passes on to another flesh that can wear it for yet a little while. ... He gazed at this familiar part of his own body, and for the first time in his life he understood that he would die.[44]

While readers of this passage will have no difficulty in describing Castorp's experience as one that has taught him something about the meaning of death, it is important to note that this is not because of anything in the X-ray itself, which might, or might not, have had this edifying effect. Mann brings this out in the reaction of Hofrat Behrens, a man of science well acquainted with the sight of skeletons, who merely remarks: 'Spooky, what? Yes, there's something distinctly spooky about it.'[45] It is quite possible that Behrens was himself moved by his first perception of an X-ray of his own body, similarly to the way that Castorp is moved by his. We are not told, nor does it matter.

What does matter is that here is a good example of how the familiar ('this familiar part of his own body') can open up new avenues of understanding, if it is looked at from a new perspective, in a different light. This is what is literally true in the case of Castorp, who 'sees' his mortality in a way that is at the same time a deepened understanding. What produces in Castorp this 'sudden enlightenment' is the contrast between the transient (temporal) and the enduring (eternal), on the one hand, and that between individuality and impersonality, on the other. His grandfather's signet ring and the 'flesh in which he moved' constitute the former contrast, while the difference between the uniquely individuating features of his personality and the corporeality in which these are expressed, as well as that paradigm of impersonality and common symbol of death – his skeleton – enter into the other. The terrifying aspect of Castorp's experience, however, can edify through the thought that, in death, all are equal – a realisation which fosters in him a greater sense of fellowship with other human beings. Moreover, Castorp realises that his life has whatever significance it has solely against the background of his mortality. Some may find it surprising that such a recognition should take place 'under the auspices of physical science', that science may itself provide an opportunity, not just for amazement and wonder, but for the kind of understanding that Castorp has acquired, both of his own mortality and that of others.

But *that* Castorp's look at his X-ray should have had this effect is, of course, not independent of the considerable intellectual, emotional and spiritual sensibilities Mann ascribes to him. Mann's introduction of the young Castorp as 'an ordinary man'[46] is deliberately ironic, as we soon learn that he possesses quite unusual powers of discernment and observation, and hence the kind of disinterested attentiveness that Weil thinks a precondition of spiritual depth. In the absence of these characteristics, Castorp might have looked at the skeleton of his hand and found the sight amazing, perhaps even 'spooky', without its impressing him the way it does now. That would have been a different kind of amazement, a different kind of wonder, and it would not have made the kind of difference to his life that it does make.

For shortly after the X-ray, Castorp's conduct changes. Contrary to all custom at the Berghof, he spontaneously decides to devote at least some of his time to the moribund, to the terminally ill who have but a few weeks to live. Addressing his cousin Joachim, whom he has come to visit at the sanatorium, he says:

> We live up here, next door to the dying, close to misery and suffering; and not only do we act as though we had nothing to do with it, but it is all carefully arranged in order to spare us and prevent our coming into contact with it, or seeing anything at all – they will take away the gentleman rider while we are at breakfast or tea – and that I find immoral. The Stöhr woman was furious, simply because I mentioned his death. That's too absurd for words. She is ignorant, to be sure, ... but even so, she might have a little human feeling, and the rest of them too. Well, I have made up my mind to concern myself a bit in future with the severe cases and the moribund.[47]

In the light of *what* the X-ray episode has taught Castorp, his subsequent behaviour towards the moribund, in particular, becomes intelligible, which it would not be if all that Castorp had learnt was that it was 'spooky' to look at an X-ray of a human hand. On the contrary, the narrative itself makes it clear that Castorp's primary motive for visiting the moribund is the fact that he wants to take suffering and death seriously, which he thinks Frau Stöhr and most other patients at the Berghof do not:

Hans Castorp went to view the gentleman rider's mortal remains. He did this of set purpose, to show his contempt for the prevailing system of secrecy, to protest against the egotistic policy of seeing and hearing nothing of such events; to register by his act his disapproval of the others' practice. He had tried to introduce the subject of the death at table, but was met with such a flat and callous rebuff on all sides as both to anger and embarrass him. Frau Stöhr had been downright gruff. What did he mean by introducing such a subject – what kind of upbringing had he had? The house regulations protected the patients from having such things come to their knowledge; and now there was this young whipper-snapper bringing it up at table, and even in the presence of Dr. Blumenkohl, whom the same fate might any day overtake (this behind her hand). If it happened again, she would complain.[48]

Mann's fine portrayal of Castorp's deepened understanding of mortality also brings out that the *moribundi* at the Berghof are really representatives of humanity at large, and that we, too, ought to give our neighbour the kind of attention that Castorp gives to the terminally ill. One of the obstacles that may get in the way of the sort of understanding Castorp has gained is thrown into relief by the character of Frau Stöhr, whom Mann describes as follows: 'Caroline Stöhr was dreadful. . . . She adored expressions of a cheap and common stamp, worn threadbare by over-use, which got on Castorp's nerves. . . . She had a boundless appetite for gossip.'[49]

Frau Stöhr's indulgence in cliché betrays a kind of inattention; her gossip, lack of consideration for others, as well as self-importance; her refusal to talk about death at table, a kind of self-deception. As Weil recognised, genuine attention to the suffering of others is a rare phenomenon, partly because of a deep-seated psychological tendency to respond to it with denial – we exaggerate our own suffering and belittle that of others, hold the afflicted responsible for their own fate, etc. – and partly because such attention involves the painful recognition that one's own position *vis-à-vis* the afflicted is merely the product of chance:

Not only does the love of God have attention for its substance; the love of our neighbour, which we know to be the same love, is made of the same substance. Those who are unhappy have no need for anything in this world but people capable of giving them their attention. The capacity to give one's attention to a sufferer is a very rare and difficult thing; it is almost a miracle; it *is* a miracle. Nearly all those who think they have this capacity do not possess it.[50]

Recalling what was said earlier about Kleist and Weil's conceptions of truth, Mann's example shows that what Castorp understands is not illuminatingly described by saying that he comes to believe the proposition that all men are mortal. That all men are mortal, and that he is one of them, is something he knew even before his experience in the examination room, as Mann's account of Castorp's childhood illustrates. Thus, we are told that, when Castorp was young, death was a familiar fact in his life, an occurrence which played chiefly 'on the senses of the lad',[51] and which caused him some emotional discomfort, but otherwise occupied him little. Both of his parents died between his fifth and seventh birthdays, and even his grandfather, who then took the young Castorp into his house, only lived for another eighteen months. The young Castorp, while registering death as a fact, does not yet understand its meaning.

It is tempting to think that, in the case of the young, such detachment from the meaning of death is not surprising, but that it will hardly be found in the more mature, let alone in the old, who are bound to learn Castorp's lesson soon enough. But this would be a hasty conclusion, as the case of Adolf Eichmann shows.[52] Shortly before his execution, Hannah Arendt reports,

> he began by stating emphatically that he was a *Gottgläubiger* [believer in God], to express in common Nazi fashion that he was no Christian and did not believe in life after death. He then proceeded: 'After a short while, gentlemen, we shall all meet again. Such is the fate of all men. Long live Germany, long live Argentina.' In the face of death he found the cliché used in funeral oratory. Under the gallows his memory played him the last trick; he was elated and he forgot that this was his own funeral.[53]

Eichmann's case is similar to that of the young Castorp in that Eichmann's failure to understand the meaning of his own death is not properly described as a blindness to the fact that humans are mortal. As Raimond Gaita puts it: 'He did not forget that Adolf Eichmann was being executed and that he was Adolf Eichmann. The reality from which he was estranged was not the *fact* of his death but its *meaning*.'[54] Gaita's point about Eichmann's inability to speak deeply about death, or, as I should like to put it, his inability to do so with the sort of understanding that is revealed in the remark of the enlightened Castorp, is not a hasty one. It is made against the background of considerations that go well beyond Eichmann's funeral speech and concern his general character, such as his boastfulness – 'I will jump into my grave laughing, because the fact that I have the death of five million Jews on my conscience gives me extraordinary satisfaction';[55] his egocentrism; his almost systematic disregard for the truth; his predilection for slogans, platitudes, and the use of the same stock phrases and self-invented clichés.[56]

As Arendt, who was present at the trial and had an opportunity to study Eichmann at first hand, perceptively remarks, his speech was a perfect expression of a more general moral failing, and one that Weil would see as a paradigm of inattention: 'The longer one listened to him, the more obvious it became that his inability to speak was closely connected with an inability to *think*, namely, to think from the standpoint of somebody else.'[57] A good illustration of Eichmann's inability to respond attentively to affliction is the story of his encounter with an unfortunate Jewish functionary, Kommerzialrat Storfer, with whom he had once collaborated. One day, Eichmann received a telegram from Rudolf Höss, the commandant of Auschwitz, informing him that Storfer had arrived and that he had urgently requested to see Eichmann. According to Eichmann, 'I said to myself: O.K., this man has always behaved well, that is worth my while ... I'll go there myself and see what is the matter with him.'[58] On arrival, Eichmann was told that Storfer had made the mistake of going into hiding, had been caught and arrested, and could certainly not be let out of the camp. Content with this explanation, Eichmann then went to speak to Storfer himself:

With Storfer afterward, well, it was a normal and human, we had a normal, human encounter. He told me all his grief and sorrow: I said: 'Well, my dear old friend, we certainly got it! What rotten luck!' And I also said: 'Look, I really cannot help you, because of orders from the Reichsführer nobody can get out' ... I forget what his reply to this was. And then I asked him how he was. And he said, yes, he wondered if he couldn't be let off work, it was heavy work. And then I said to Höss: 'Work – Storfer won't have to work!' But Höss said: 'Everyone works here.' So I said:

'O.K.' I said, 'I'll make out a chit to the effect that Storfer has to keep the gravel paths in order with a broom ... and that he has the right to sit down with his broom on one of the benches.' [To Storfer] I said: 'Will that be all right, Mr Storfer, will that suit you?' Whereupon he was very pleased, and we shook hands. ... It was a great inner joy to me that I could at least see the man with whom I had worked for so many long years, and that we could speak with each other.[59]

Six weeks later, Storfer was shot. In the light of Eichmann's psychological profile and general moral attitude towards the victims of his crimes, it is hard not to read his account of the meeting with Storfer – he called it 'a normal human encounter' – as a case of self-delusion, as the exact opposite, in fact, of what Weil identifies as true love of one's neighbour:

The love of our neighbour in all its fullness simply means being able to say to him: 'What are you going through?' It is a recognition that the sufferer exists, not only as a unit in a collection, or a specimen from the social category labeled 'unfortunate', but as a man, exactly like us, who was one day stamped with a special mark by affliction. For this reason it is enough, but it is indispensable, to know how to look at him in a certain way.[60]

A more accurate description of Eichmann's meeting with Storfer would be that of an encounter between someone in power and an unlucky Jew who had been a useful instrument in the Nazis' terrible scheme. Eichmann never wavered in his blind obedience to orders from above, nor can the chit he made out for Storfer appear as anything other than a self-congratulatory gesture, undertaken to reaffirm to himself his view that he, too, had power and influence. It is both interesting and ironic, though Weil would not find this surprising, that a fine humanist education like Castorp's should culminate in precisely the sort of attention that Eichmann lacks, not only with regard to other human beings, but in relation to the meaning of mortality. On the latter issue, Weil says: 'Death is the most precious thing that has been given to man. That is why the supreme impiety is to make an improper use of it.'[61]

As the example of Castorp illustrates, there is an internal connection between a given conception of death, on the one hand, and one's relation to the value of life – one's own and that of others – on the other. If Eichmann has made 'an improper use of it', it is not only because, when the Reverend William Hull offered to read the Scriptures with him, the self-professed 'Gottgläubiger' declined the offer on the grounds that he had only two hours to live, and therefore 'no time to waste';[62] it is also because Eichmann's last words, far from echoing Weil's contention that 'one must accept death entirely as annihilation',[63] turned out to be little more than a see-you-later vulgarisation of the concept.[64]

The above comparisons between Kleist, Weil, the Curé d'Ars, and Castorp on the one hand, and Eichmann and Frau Stöhr on the other, naturally prompt more general questions about the relation between school/university education and the prevention of evil. In the light of Weil's remarks on the intellectually and morally purifying nature of true attention, it is tempting to think that a humanistic or religious education conducted in the spirit of such attention would constitute a powerful prophylactic against such evil as Eichmann has committed. Given the role that Simone Weil assigns to grace, however, such a claim would clearly be too strong. Even if school studies are being put to good use – in Weil's sense – the education of the young is always conducted under the banner of hope, and thus in the realisation that the persistence of the attention in question depends just as much on grace as it does on personal effort.

3

A Philosophical
Apprenticeship

A. From mathematics to philosophy

An account of Simone Weil's spiritual development would be seriously deficient if it did not also speak of her *philosophical* education, and of the way in which philosophical reflection continued to
shape her thoughts on moral, political, and religious matters. As we
have already seen, the crisis which she experienced at the age of
fourteen involved far more than a sense of intellectual inadequacy
vis-à-vis her brother's mathematical genius. What troubled her was
not so much the prospect of being unable to solve particular problems of mathematics as 'the idea of being excluded from that
transcendent kingdom ... wherein truth abides' – the thought, in
other words, that her passionate quest for the truth would be for
ever thwarted by the limitations of her cognitive abilities. For
someone whose whole being is wrapped up in such a quest, the
prospect of inevitable failure is not merely frustrating, but deeply
unsettling. This is why Weil could plausibly affirm that 'I preferred
to die rather than live without that truth', and why she went
through 'months of inward darkness' before she was suddenly
struck by the conviction that nobody is barred from attaining to
wisdom, 'if only he longs for truth and perpetually concentrates all
his *attention* on its attainment'.

38

At the time of these thoughts, in 1923/24, Weil was still preparing for the first part of her baccalaureate (in Latin and Greek), and had not yet embarked on a rigorous, academic study of philosophy. Even so, her reference to mathematics as a 'transcendent kingdom' of truth, and her hint at the more general questions about the scope and limits of human understanding that go hand in hand with it, already reveal a fine philosophical sensibility in her thinking, and a curiosity that is more than intellectual.

But why, one might ask, should one ever think of mathematics as 'transcendent', and of its subject matter as a 'kingdom' of truth? When we add up our monthly expenses or pay for our shopping at the local grocery store, we certainly trust that the sums are accurate and the results of our calculations true. But is this truth any more 'transcendent' than numbers and equations scribbled on a notepad? Mathematics seems to be a useful tool for keeping track of our bank balances, designing a building, measuring the size of a cornfield, or steering a ship through the ocean, but what is sublime about the calculations that are involved in these activities? Weil would certainly agree that there is nothing mysterious or transcendent about mathematical calculation per se, just as she would accept the view that mathematics must not detach itself from human life in a way that reduces its subject matter to a kind of intellectual game. On the other hand, a purely pragmatic and wholly instrumental conception of mathematics would have seemed to her not only superficial and crude, but *spiritually* impoverished. In his excellent memoir *Uncle Tungsten*, the American neurologist Oliver Sacks provides us with an example of a very different attitude towards the world of numbers, and one that also gets us closer to Weil's thought:

My father was a whiz at mental arithmetic, and I, too, even at the age of six, was quick with figures – and more, in love with them. I liked numbers because they were solid, invariant; they stood unmoved in a chaotic world. There was in numbers and their relation something absolute, certain, not to be questioned, beyond doubt. ... I particularly loved prime numbers, the fact that they were indivisible, could not be broken down, were inalienably themselves. (I had no such confidence in myself, for I felt I was being divided, alienated, broken down, more every week.) Primes were the building blocks of all other numbers, and there must be, I felt, some meaning to them. Why did primes come when they did? Was there any pattern, any logic to their distribution? Was there any limit to them, or did they go on forever?[1]

Like Sacks, Weil was struck by the peculiar *necessity* that governs the relations between numbers, a necessity which also allowed one to speak of mathematical truths as paradigms of knowledge and certainty. The nature of this necessity reveals itself in the fact that we take such statements as '2 + 2 = 4' to be no more open to doubt or dispute than the properties of the geometrical figures which the demented Nietzsche reportedly drew in the sand outside an asylum in Jena. These properties could be said to be 'transcendent' in the sense that they do not depend on anything in the physical world, on what a philosopher might do with a wooden stick in the grounds of a German hospital, for example. So, while the mathematical pragmatist we mentioned earlier is quite right to insist that there is nothing mysterious about sums scribbled on a piece of paper, or geometrical shapes drawn in the sand, the mathematical or geometrical truths expressed *in* these sums or shapes could still be said to be 'transcendent'. In what sense, though?

We may grant that the properties of a triangle, say, are not subjective projections of the human intellect, but genuine discoveries about an independent reality. But then, what does the phrase 'independent reality' amount to? One possible answer might be that mathematical and geometrical objects, including prime numbers, circles, and triangles, are *metaphysical* entities which exist, quite literally, in an immaterial and timeless world of their own, and that the sums in our notebooks and the geometrical proofs in textbooks of geometry are only the *physical* representations of these entities and their relations. But now, are we even clear about what a 'literal' existence of such timeless entities would mean? And what, exactly, would be the nature of the connection between those ephemeral metaphysical existents on the one hand, and the robust, physical environment in which we lead our daily lives, on the other? Clearly, all these questions are *philosophical* questions, and there has been a great deal of controversy, not only about how they should be answered, but about the extent to which they are even intelligible questions to begin with.

I won't join in that controversy now, save to note that the remarks I quoted above from Weil and Sacks do not present a *philosophical theory* about the nature of numbers, triangles, and mathematico-geometrical relations. Thus far, they merely record a certain kind of wonder at the existence of such things, a pre-theo-retical response to a puzzling aspect of a perfectly familiar feature of human life. One has to *see* the phenomenon in a certain light, of course, and be struck by it in a particular way, for the experience to invite deeper reflection. In Oliver Sacks' case, that reflection was carried an important step further by the way in which his aunt proceeded to relate the world of mathematics to that of sunflowers, pine cones, snail shells, and similarly concrete objects in Sacks' experience of nature:

> She showed me the spiral patterns on the faces of sunflowers in the garden, and suggested I count the florets in these. As I did so, she pointed out that they were arranged according to a series – 1, 1, 2, 3, 5, 8, 13, 21, etc. – each number being the sum of the two that preceded it. And if one divided each number by the number that followed it (1/2, 2/3, 3/5, 5/8, etc.) one approached the number 0.618. This series, she said, was called a Fibonacci series, after an Italian mathematician who had lived centuries before. The ratio of 0.618, she added, was known as the divine pro-portion or the golden section, an ideal geometrical proportion often used by architects and artists. . . . She had me look at fallen pinecones, to see that they, too, had spirals based on the golden section.[2]

What Sacks learnt from his aunt – and, analogously, Weil from her brother André – was that there exists an intimate connection between, on the one hand, the timeless harmony and proportion in the realm of numbers, and the structure of the natural world, on the other, and that this connection could inspire both wonder and, in those who had the proper kind of sensibility, a sense of the trans-cendent: if the spiral structure of a fallen pine cone, for example, is expressible in terms of the mathematical ratio known as the golden section, and if the latter is itself a kind of timeless ideal, then our very experience of the material world already gestures beyond itself! Indeed, as Oliver Sacks' examples illustrate, it would be more appropriate to speak of mathematics as being both transcendent over, and immanent in, the world of everyday experience. This way of putting it may sound paradoxical, not to say contradictory, but it also seems to be the most natural way to describe the phenomenon.

Now, the notions of immanence and transcendence also figure prominently in religious discourse, where they inform an analogous paradox concerning God's relation to the world – he, too, is said to be both immanent in, and transcendent over, the world – and it is crucial for a proper understanding of Simone Weil's view of mathematics that her remarks on the subject be read against the background of this very analogy. In her view, it is not surprising that those who have gained a particularly deep understanding of numerical and geometrical relations should want to speak of certain ratios as 'golden', 'ideal', or 'divine', and that they should invest these ratios with a spiritual significance akin to religious belief, since that is precisely the significance they do have. Once again, the genealogy of Oliver Sacks' growing love and appreciation of mathematics, mediated as it was through his aunt's religious outlook, also shows something about the evolution of Weil's own thoughts on the subject. Sacks continues:

> The association of plants, gardens, with numbers assumed a curiously intense, symbolic form for me. I started to think in terms of a kingdom or realm of numbers, with its own geography, languages, and laws. ... Among my friends in this garden were not only primes and Fibonacci sunflowers, but perfect numbers (such as 6 or 28, the sum of their factors, excluding themselves); Pythagorean numbers, whose square was the sum of two other squares (such as 3, 4, 5, or 5, 12, 13); and 'amicable numbers' (such as 220 and 284), pairs of numbers in which the factors each added up to the other. And my aunt had shown me that my garden of numbers was doubly magical – not just delightful and friendly, always there, but part of the plan on which the whole universe was built. Numbers, my aunt said, are the way God thinks.[3]

The thought of mathematics as a bridge between the temporal and the eternal; the recognition that the visible universe is governed by necessities which reflect the immutable nature of something that transcends it; and the implications of this recognition for human action – all this had already begun to engage Weil's thoughts as early as 1925, when she was still deliberating about whether to take the second part of her baccalaureate examinations in mathematics or philosophy, and these ideas continued to inform her reflections on mathematics right up until 1942. In the new Gallimard edition of her *Cahiers* – of the projected four volumes, three have already been published – one can see much more clearly than in the incomplete, English edition of 1956 how important the subject was to her. Each volume contains frequent references to it, as well as numerous and often highly complex mathematical equations and geometrical drawings, interspersed with more general reflections on the value of mathematics as an instrument of spiritual growth.

However, a more accessible and less technical treatment of the matter is found in Weil's essay 'The Pythagorean Doctrine', written in the autumn of 1941 and reprinted in *Intimations of Christianity among the Ancient Greeks*, as well as in some of the letters she wrote to her brother André at around the same time. Here, she sets out more fully why she thinks of mathematics as a bridge between God and man, and why the Pythagorean legacy, in particular, is to be understood as a richly insightful intimation of such key religious concepts as incarnation, mediation, and transcendence.Weil admits that we can only speculate that

> perhaps from the beginning of time men have regarded whole numbers as appropriate to serve as images of the divine truths because of their perfect precision, because of the certainty, and at the same time the mystery, contained in their relationships[4]

but she is quick to point out that 'the link between mathematical preoccupation on the one hand and philosophico-religious pre-occupation on the other is historically confirmed for the age of Pythagoras'.[5] As one would expect, Weil's continuous fascination with Pythagoras and his followers goes well beyond an academic interest in their contributions to mathematics and geometry – the classification of integers as odd, even, prime, and composite; the Pythagorean theorem, according to which the square on the hypotenuse of a right-angled triangle is equal to the sum of the squares on the other sides ($c^2 = a^2 + b^2$); the incommensurability of the side and the diagonal of a square; the definition of a 'perfect' number as one that equals the sum of all its proper divisors (e.g. $6 = 1 + 2 + 3$); and the discovery that musical intervals can be expressed as numerical proportions, for example. What intrigued her about these insights was not simply their content and the fact that they increased the stock of mathematico-geometrical knowledge, but the *spirit* of the enquiries that made them possible, and the way in which they were taken up into the lives of those who celebrated these discoveries.

As Weil was well aware, the Pythagoreans were not only mathematicians, but members of a religious brotherhood – founded by Pythagoras in southern Italy, around 532 BC – whose intellectual and practical endeavours revolved around the idea of salvation through purification of the soul and a life lived in harmony with the cosmos. None of Pythagoras' writings have survived, but we know that novices to his community had to observe secrecy and silence with regard to holy matters, take vows of abstinence, obedience, and piety, and exercise modesty and self-discipline in their daily lives. The mathematical explorations of the Pythagoreans did not take place *in vacuo*, then, but within the context of a distinctly *religious* attitude; an attitude which not only fuelled their desire to penetrate more deeply into the mysteries of the cosmos in which they found themselves, but also required them to manifest in their own lives the very principles of proportion and harmony which they found in the realm of numbers. This is why, for Weil, the Pythagoreans are a superb example of how the study of mathematics can itself become a means of *purification*. As she puts it in a letter to her brother André:

> Purity of soul was their one concern; to 'imitate God' was the secret of it; the imitation of God was assisted by the study of mathematics, in so far as one conceived the whole universe to be subject to mathematical law, which made the geometer an imitator of the supreme lawgiver.[6]

The Pythagoreans' primary reason for studying numerical relations, ratios, and theorems was thus an ethico-religious one. They saw in mathematics an expression of the divine law or *logos* which governed the cosmos, and in the idea of *proportion*, the key to a life lived *in imitatio Dei*. According to Weil, the idea of proportion had thus become 'the theme of a meditation' which had the power to transform the soul.[7] She says:

> In the eyes of the Greeks, the very principle of the soul's salvation was measure, balance, proportion, harmony; because desire is always unmeasured and boundless. Therefore, to conceive the universe as an equilibrium and a harmony, is to make it like a mirror of salvation.[8]

For the Greeks, a man's soul was permanently at risk of being corrupted by submission to desires and inclinations that drew him away from the good, and therefore prone to a state of disequilibrium in which he was simultaneously out of tune with himself and the cosmos at large. Examples of this condition would be a man who knows what is morally required of him, but who is nevertheless too weak-willed to act as he should, or someone who selfishly fulfils his every desire without showing any regard for the well-being of others. The first character reveals a striking incongruence between thought and action; the second, a disproportionate regard for the self, and a distorted sense of justice in his relation to others. Both agents – and the second more than the first – need to redress this imbalance in their souls, and endeavour to transform themselves in such a way that their actions not only accord with the good, but flow from their characters with the same *necessity* that governs the proof of a mathematical or geometrical theorem. In her *Spiritual Autobiography*, Simone Weil expresses this point by saying that 'the most beautiful life possible has always seemed to me to be one ... where there is never any room for choice',[9] by which she means that a life lived truly *in imitatio Dei* would be one in which the relation between understanding God's will and doing it would not merely be contingent, but *necessary*.

The biblical story of the Good Samaritan (Luke 10.29–37), who neither hesitates nor deliberates, but simply helps his afflicted neighbour without a second thought, is a good example of what Weil has in mind when she speaks of the ideal life as one 'where there is never any room for choice'. Obviously, she is not denying that human beings are free to choose what they want to do. In Luke's parable, the priest and the Levite are not acting under any kind of compulsion when they decide to ignore their neighbour, but out of their own free will. Nor is Weil suggesting, even more implausibly, that the most beautiful life would be one in which there was no deliberation or reflection. Her point is rather that, in the sphere of moral actions, the relation between an agent and his deeds should imitate the relation between God's unchanging will and his creation. Only then can these actions be said to be truly good and, in so far as they manifest a certain kind of necessity and inevitability, beautiful.

To see this point more clearly, one only needs to contrast Luke's Samaritan with one who also decides to help, but only after he has reflected on whether he can afford to delay his journey, and wondered how much it is going to inconvenience him. Such a Samaritan would still have done the right thing, but he clearly wouldn't have served Luke's purpose, which was to show that a genuine love of neighbour silences such deliberations and that, in so silencing them, it becomes a model of spontaneous and perfect obedience to God's will. In her discussion of the Pythagorean doctrine, therefore, Weil finds it quite natural to liken the moral integrity of a good man to the 'fidelity' revealed in geometrical relations:

There is an analogy between the fidelity of the right-angled triangle to the relationship which forbids it to emerge from the circle of which its hypotenuse is the diameter, and that of a man who, for example, abstains from the acquisition of power or of money at the price of fraud. The first may be regarded as a perfect example of the second.[10]

The value of the analogy consists in showing something about the nature of moral integrity, and about the force and sense of such expressions as 'I *must* help him', 'I *cannot* betray her', etc., namely, that the necessities and impossibilities expressed in these exclamations are just as absolute and unconditional as the laws of mathematics and geometry. The conception of the ethical as a realm of *absolute* and unconditional value is, of course, an essential aspect of the Christian tradition, where the moral law is seen as divine command, and its transgression is simultaneously seen as a violation of God's will. In so far as Pythagorean thought, that 'great mystery of Greek civilization',[11] shares this conception of absolute value and sees in mathematical necessity a *mediator* between the earthly and the divine, one can also speak of it as an intimation of a central feature of the Christian faith:

> Just as the Christ is, on one hand, the mediation between God and man, and on the other the mediator between man and his neighbour, so mathematical necessity is on one hand the mediator between God and things, and on the other between each thing and every other thing.[12]

Meditating on the Pythagoreans' discovery of the proportional mean – a value b such that $a:b$ equals $b:c$ – Weil is struck by the way in which it foreshadows Christian reflections on the relation between God, Christ, his disciples, and the saints:

> 'As my Father hath sent me, even so I send you, etc.' A single relationship unites the Father to Christ, Christ to His disciples. Christ is the proportional mean between God and the saints. The very word mediation indicates this.[13]

Having charted the development of Weil's thoughts on mathematics from the time of her adolescent crisis in 1923 to her essay on Pythagoras in 1941, one can see more clearly why she holds the study of mathematics in such high regard. Provided that it is conducted in the right spirit, and its revelations are properly meditated upon, it can both draw one towards a religious conception of the world and, as the example of the Pythagorean brotherhood demonstrates, serve as a means of spiritual purification. What the Pythagoreans managed to do, in other words, was to walk that precariously thin tightrope between treating mathematics as a source of purely abstract, intellectual stimulation on the one hand, and seeing in it no more than a powerful tool for the solution of practical problems, on the other. For them, meditation on a theorem had the same existential significance as the contemplation of the divine mysteries was to have for later generations of religious believers, and it required the same kind of *attention* that, according to Weil, is also characteristic of serious prayer.

Now most contemporary readers of Weil's work, including those who would describe themselves as devout Christians, might admit that these reflections make a valuable contribution to our understanding of the genealogy of Christian thought from Pythagoras to the New Testament, but would they not also find it hard to look at geometry and mathematics in quite the way the Pythagoreans did – to know what it would mean, for example, to celebrate the discovery of a geometrical axiom with a religious feast? David McLellan has plausibly suggested that 'Weil is more certain about the essence of Pythagorean thought than anyone else has managed to be',[14] and it is tempting to think that her superior grasp of Pythagoreanism must therefore be the result of her extensive mathematical training. This inference would be hasty, though, as it overlooks the religious dimension of Weil's very attitude towards mathematical enquiry. As Rush Rhees points out:

> Much of what Weil writes about necessity, about the use of mathematics in the study of science, the study of what things are, how they are related to one another, much of this is an expression of something which could not be understood except in someone who had known the grace of God as she did. It needs not only religious faith, but a kind of religious insight, in order to understand the phrases or the figures or the grammar of what she writes.[15]

Weil is, of course, well aware of this. In correspondence with her brother, she admits that 'intellectual curiosity cannot give one contact with the thought of Pythagoras ... because in regard to thought of that kind knowledge and adhesion are one single act of mind'.[16] There is a depth to Pythgorean thought that 'cannot be perceived except from inside; that is to say, only if one has truly drawn spiritual life from the texts studied'.[17]

Weil herself did draw such spiritual life from her studies, even to the point of being able to see in the appearance of geometry 'the most dazzling of all the prophecies which foretold the Christ'.[18] That most of her contemporary readers will find it difficult to follow her in this, also shows why Weil's reflections on the Pythagoreans are so pertinent to our own times. Apart from telling us something about the genealogy of Christian thought, they invite us to assess the depth of our own conception of the cosmos, show how the loss of a certain perspective may lead to religious belief that is spiritually impoverished, and challenge us to think about ways in which at least a part of that perspective may be regained.

Far from being of purely academic interest, Weil's remarks on the mathematico-religious mysticism of the Pythagoreans really constitute a kind of conceptual archaeology, designed to retrieve for the contemporary Christian believer valuable sources of spiritual illumination. Just how important she thought this retrieval, comes out in a letter to Déodet Roché in 1941:

> Never has the revival of this kind of thought been so necessary as today. We are living at a time when most people feel, confusedly but keenly, that what was called enlightenment in the 18th century, including the sciences, provides an insufficient spiritual diet; but this feeling is now leading humanity into the darkest paths. There is an urgent need to refer back to those great epochs which favoured the kind of spiritual life of which all that is most precious in science and art is no more than a somewhat imperfect reflection.[19]

Weil realises that it takes a certain atmosphere and environment for the spirit to find its proper nourishment, and even though she hopes that mathematicians will gradually return to the kind of rigour and reverential disinterestedness that, in her view, disappeared with the Greek geometers, she also has the feeling 'that our tendency today is rather towards ... mathematics as a game, more than as an art', and seriously wonders 'how many mathematicians today regard mathematics as a method for purifying the soul and imitating God'.[20] That such mathematicians are few in number, Weil attributes just as much to the demystification of mathematics as to 'the indifference which, since the Renaissance, science has shown for the spiritual life',[21] so her observations on mathematics also raise critical questions about the self-understanding of modern science, which has likewise ceased to appear as 'a special reflection of the beauty of the world'.[22] Weil finds 'something diabolic' in this whole development, but remains convinced that divine providence 'preserves mathematics from being drowned in mere technique', so that it may still serve as an introduction to the mysteries of faith.[23]

As for Pythagoreanism, she is in no doubt that we would understand a great deal more about it today, if the Roman Empire had not caused its disappearance. 'What ruined Pythagoreanism', according to Weil, 'was ... the wholesale massacre of Pythagoreans in Magna Graecia',[24] and a cultural environment that remained 'obstinately deaf' to the spiritual treasures of this and similarly esoteric cults.[25] Weil's essay on the Pythagoreans is a serious attempt to unearth these treasures, and to show how a proper conception of mathematics can also lead to a deeper understanding of the relation between God and man. In so far as Weil's reflections on this subject combine religious sensibility with philosophical perspicacity, her 1941 essay on the Pythagoreans also stands as impressive testimony to the value of the rigorous philosophical training on which she embarked in 1924, when she decided to take the second part of her baccalaureate in philosophy, and then to pursue her studies further at the Lycée Henri IV, under the tutelage of Alain. As was noted in Chapter 1, the encounter with Alain played an important role in the formation of Weil's early thought, and therefore deserves further comment.

B. The influence of Alain

When the prestigious, three-volume Pléiade edition of Alain's collected works appeared in 1956, just five years after his death, the poet André Maurois (1885–1967) described it in his prefatory note as 'one of the finest books in the world', and placed it 'in the same league as Montaigne and Montesquieu', whose style and critical outlook are very similar to Alain's own.[26] The Pléiade edition comprises more than 3,000 pages of text and is still in print today, though hardly any of it has been translated into English. Encountering Alain's writings for the first time, one is struck by their unusual format: countless miniature essays or *propos* (roughly translated as 'conversation' or 'talk'), typically less than three pages in length. The *propos* grew partly out of the work rountine Alain had set for himself, viz. to write two unrevised pages at any one sitting, and partly out of his conviction that this format was more likely to do justice to his concerns than the lengthy and often abstract treatises of the academic establishment, with their tendency to force even the most disparate phenomena into some general theoretical framework or other. Alain himself compared his *propos* to the stretto at the end of a fugue – a musical device in which the different voices are drawn together, 'as if they were passing through a ring' – and thought of it as a condensed exercise in conceptual analysis. In addition, it was a timely reaction against 'the present state of letters', which he insisted had been 'emptied of all richness and force',[27] and therefore needed to be restored to its proper status. One could say that this dual purpose sprang from the recognition that clarity of thought goes hand in hand with a serious and disciplined attention to language and the meanings of our words, and since Alain was writing for the educated reader no less than for the philosophically trained academic, his critical efforts were ultimately grounded in 'a lively political passion',[28] a strong sense of the ethical and socio-political responsibilities of the writer.

Simone Weil not only shares this attitude and attributes to the great works of literature – especially those of Homer, Aeschylus, Sophocles, Shakespeare, Racine, Molière, and Villon – at least as much power to enlighten us about the human condition as she does to rigorous philosophical reflection, but also sees a direct connection between the fate of words and the deterioration of value:

> The fate of words is a touchstone of the progressive weakening of the idea of value, and although the fate of words does not depend upon writers, one cannot help attributing a special responsibility to them, since words are their business.[29]

Among the examples Weil uses to illustrate her point, she mentions the increasing tendency towards abstraction, especially in the realm of politics, where such expressions as 'nation', 'capitalism', 'communism', 'order', 'security', 'property', and 'democracy' have become common currency without carrying a clear sense,[30] as well as the cheapening of words like 'virtue', 'nobility', 'honour', 'honesty', and 'generosity' through their application to contexts that no longer have anything to do with the appraisal of character.[31] By way of example, Weil observes that between a poem by Valéry and an advertisement for a beauty cream promising a rich marriage to anyone who used it, there was at no point a break of continuity. So as a result of literature's spiritual usurpation a beauty cream advertisement possessed, in the eyes of little village girls, the authority that was formerly attached to the words of priests.[32]

Writers, especially when they have acquired the status of celebrities, enjoy a great deal of social prestige and, thanks to their facility with words, are able to exert a considerable influence on the thoughts of their readers. Hence Alain's concern about language and the need to counteract the very tendencies Weil articulates in the above quotation. Having found in the *propos* the ideal medium for the fixing of his thoughts, Alain continued to produce well over 5,000 of these philosophical vignettes in the period 1903–36 alone, and published many of them in his own journal, *Libres propos*, from 1921 onwards. They cover a wide array of topics, with titles ranging from 'The Apostle Paul', 'The Tragedians', and 'The Artist and the Profession', through 'Human Rights', 'Fidelity', and 'Rites', to 'Geometry and Latin', 'Sleeping', and 'Thoughts on Ozone'.

While Weil does not adopt this format for her own reflections, she does approve of its underlying motivation and sees her essays as similarly open-ended exercises in conceptual clarification, rather than as attempts at systematisation or theory-building. This concern with the relation between *form* and *content*, with finding the right *voice* in the formulation of one's thoughts, especially in relation to matters of spiritual and other kinds of value, is by no means peripheral to Alain's and Weil's philosophical endeavours. They realised that there was a strong temptation to model non-scientific modes of discourse on the structural and stylistic templates dictated by the natural sciences, and that the failure to resist that temptation invariably generated conceptual confusion and, by implication, a certain kind of superficiality in thought and feeling. Here, literature can serve as a powerful corrective, and it is not surprising, therefore, that Alain always insisted on teaching it alongside philosophy – a practice Simone Weil continued to adopt in her own teaching as well. Thus, she would write and talk about Homer, the Greek tragedians Aeschylus and Sophocles, Shakespeare, Racine, Molière, Villon, and Stendhal, in particular, not only because 'those poets had genius', but because 'it was a genius oriented towards the good'.[33]

But the love of literature which she shared with Alain also coloured her understanding of philosophy. Intrigued by Leonardo's reflections on the philosophical dimension of painting, she finds that the philosopher, too, must express his thoughts creatively and 'make a work of art ... with words'.[34] Weil writes:

The idea of painting having a connection with philosophy is not a new idea for us if we have read Leonardo da Vinci. Leonardo may have been the only one in our tradition to say that painting is a philosophy that uses lines and colors, but possibly he was not the only one to think so. Can real art be anything but a method of establishing a certain relationship between the world and the self, between oneself and the self, that is, the equivalent of a philosophy?[35]

The list of frequently recurring themes in the philosophical writings of Alain includes the nature of human perception, value judgements, political activity, and religious belief, and it would be fair to say that Weil not only shared these interests, but found herself in agreement with much of what her teacher believed in these areas. A typical example of Alain's style of reflection is this excerpt from one of his *propos*:

Nature never ceases to prophesy. Trees, flowers, birds, insects, all advise us. The city-dweller watches the drift of the clouds or of smoke; and I know of an old woman who forecasts rain by watching her canaries; they sometimes spill water out of their dishes, and when they do it always rains. But this simple example can only mislead the imagination, for the signs turn out to be magical by coincidence. The canaries seem to speak in gestures; but in fact the little apparatus that keeps their water dishes at a constant level is a highly sensitive barometer, and the water overflows when the air pressure decreases. Thus one can tell the truth, and still be wrong. And we must note once again that experience, which is never deceptive, always deceives us.[36]

What is, and what is not, real? Is there a sense in which our own understanding of the world is analogous to that of the old woman in Alain's example – true, and yet wrong? These and similar questions no doubt stimulated Weil to embark on the long process of reflection that culminated in her essay 'Science and Perception in Descartes', the qualifying dissertation she wrote for the École

Normale Supérieure in 1929, and to take a special interest in the works of Plato and Kant, whose reflections lent further support to her belief that the concept of the real is considerably more complex than it seems. Particularly instructive in this connection is Plato's allegory of the cave, according to which most people's perspective on the world is based on a terrible and tragic misconception of how things *really* are. The allegory, presented by Socrates in Book VII of Plato's *Republic*, begins as follows:

> Imagine human beings living in an underground, cave-like dwelling, with an entrance a long way up, which is both open to the light and as wide as the cave itself. They've been there since childhood, fixed in the same place, with their necks and legs fettered, able to see only in front of them, because their bonds prevent them from turning their heads around. Light is provided by a fire burning far above and behind them. Also behind them, but on higher ground, there is a path stretching between them and the fire. Imagine that along this path a low wall has been built, like the screen in front of puppeteers above which they show their puppets.[37]

If the experience of these cave-dwellers – Socrates speaks of them as 'prisoners' – was thus constrained, then '[they] would in every way believe that the truth is nothing other than the shadows of those artifacts.'[38] Moreover, if one of them was unexpectedly freed and compelled to walk towards the light, 'he'd be pained and dazzled and unable to see the things whose shadows he'd seen before'.[39] He would find it difficult to accept, not only that there *was* something other than the shadow-play in the cave, but that his previous experiences had been entirely *dependent* on a wholly different realm of being, by comparison with which everything else is merely an appearance. The realisation that he had been living under an illusion would no doubt be painful and agonising, but it would also constitute a liberating reorientation towards the truth. If Weil sees in Plato's story of the cave 'a terrible image of human misery',[40] it is because she takes our current (spiritual) condition to be identical to that of the cave-dwellers: 'what constitutes the real essence of their misery ... is their total dependence upon the passing shadows and their error in believing that those shadows are real'.[41] The cave is the material world, the domain of space, time, causal relations, worldly needs, desires, and ambitions; the shadows on its wall, our ineradicable tendencies towards daydreaming, wishful thinking, self-deception, and idolatry. Like Plato's prisoners, so Weil notes,

> we are born and live *in passivity*. It is not we who move, but images pass before our eyes and we live them. And we make no choices. What we live at any moment is what is offered us by the puppet-master. (We are not told anything about him. ... The Prince of this world?)[42]

But how does one emerge from this seemingly natural passivity and proneness to ignorance – even about ourselves – and come to realise that things are not what they seem? Weil hints at an answer when she says that

> the chains have fallen away as soon as a human being receives – either through inspiration or by the instruction of another, whether oral or written (it is often a book) – the idea that this world is not everything, that there is something else which is better, and that one must seek.[43]

The thought that 'this world is not everything' is also the central theme of Immanuel Kant's difficult and subtle *Critique of Pure Reason*, which could be read as a sophisticated 'modern' argument for the appearance/reality distinction drawn in Plato's allegory of the cave. Like Plato, Kant holds that our experience of the world is necessarily constrained, and he identifies the 'fetters' as structural features of the mind itself, without which there could be no intelligible experience at all. These features include space, time, and causality, and allow us to perceive such things as tables, chairs, trees, and indeed our own bodies, as three-dimensional objects, embedded in a complex network of causal relations.

This does not mean, however, that the world – understood as the realm of *phenomena* – is a purely subjective creation of the human mind, such that, if there were no minds, there would be no world, either. Kant's claim is rather that, while there *is* a mind-independent reality (the *noumenal*), it is not one that could be conceptualised in spatio-temporal, causal, or any of the other terms available to the understanding. Moreover, Kant thinks that something like this perspectivism, in which phenomena and noumena are presented as two sides or aspects of one and the same existential coin, has to be true, if we are ever to attach any meaning to belief in an eternal and transcendent God. In Kant's universe, such a God exists outside space and time because human experience invariably unfolds *in* space and time, and it is precisely because God can enter the world through the noumenal door, as it were, that 'this [phenomenal] world is not everything'. The notion of the noumenal is, of course, by no means unproblematic and would require a more extensive discussion than we can afford it here. Kant himself admits, for instance, that, since the noumenal is characterised entirely negatively (non-spatial, non-temporal, non-causal, etc.), the concept of a noumenon is 'a merely *limiting concept*', whose function is to delimit the boundaries of intelligible experience and thought from within, as it were.[44]

If so, then what is one to make of God's relation to the world? In his late notebooks, Kant tells us that 'God is the creator of things in themselves',[45] whereas man is the creator of appearances,[46] which rather suggests that God is not only one, but two tiers removed from the world of those who worship him.[47] Even if these difficulties could be satisfactorily resolved and Kant's view shown to be compatible with the traditional Christian belief in a *living* God, however, it would still come under heavy fire from philosophers like Arthur Schopenhauer, who has plausibly shown – in *The World as Will and Idea* – that one might well embrace Kant's metaphysical perspectivism without thereby endorsing his theistic conclusions: the noumenal door may, indeed, be wide open, but what if there are no convincing reasons for believing that there *is* a God to walk through it? On the other hand, and in spite of his vigorously atheistic outlook on human life, Schopenhauer does acknowledge that religious believers, whether they be Christians, Jews, Muslims, Hindus, or Buddhists, have grasped an important truth about man's relation to the world, viz. that there is a sense in which his representations of it are no more than phenomenal shadows on the walls of the intellect, and that questions about the meaning and final purpose of human existence can only be answered by reference to the transcendent and metaphysical ground of our representations.

And Simone Weil? Much though she applauds Kant for the sophisticated philosophical articulation of this insight in the *Critique of Pure Reason*, her numerous references and allusions to Plato's allegory rather suggest that she considers it a superior expression of the same idea, partly because it eschews abstract and technical vocabulary, and partly because of its practical, existential import with regard to the intellectual and spiritual education of the young. As Weil puts it:

In order to direct one's attention to the perfect patterns of things, one has to stop valuing things which are always changing and not eternal. One can look at the same world, which is before our eyes, either from the point of view of its relation to time, or from that of its relationship to eternity. Education means turning the soul in the direction in which it should look, of delivering the soul from the passions.[48]

Following Plato, Weil also thinks that those whose minds have already been turned in the right direction will acknowledge their ethical and political responsibilities towards their fellow human beings:

The wise have to return to the cave, and act there. One has to reach the stage where power is in the hands of those who refuse it, and not of those whose ambition it is to possess it.[49]

Weil's philosophical and political activities, too, should be understood in the light of this practical exhortation. Like Socrates, who thought that nothing worse could befall a man than false beliefs about how one should live, and who consequently spent most of his daily life in serious conversation with the citizens of Athens, Weil gave much of her life to educating the minds and ameliorating the predicaments of those still 'imprisoned' either spiritually or physically, and she always did so without any hope for reward or personal gain.

Returning to Alain with the above in mind, we can see why his reflections on the concepts of reality and existence is particularly relevant when it comes to talking about spiritual matters:

The first and supreme paradox is that the spirit does not exist. We have strict methods for getting hold of what exists. The nets we use are ideas, and they are thrown out into experience, which, according to common sense, alone decides, provided that we question it properly. ... There is no arguing with this method. Yet these means have never located the spirit anywhere, either outside of man or within him, either in the living man or in the departure of the dead, either in the mouths of oracles or in the sanctuaries of healing.[50]

However, Alain does not conclude from this that there is no such thing as spirit. On the contrary, 'when we say that it does not exist, we mean that it is more than existence. This simple description goes beyond all the hyperboles of theology'.[51] The paradox Alain is talking about, and which we shall encounter again in Chapter 5, is analogous to the one Jules Lagneau captured in his comment on God: 'God cannot be said to exist, for he cannot be apprehended in the context of experience.'[52] God's reality, in other words, is not on a par with that of tables, chairs, trees, rocks, or anything else we might include in a list of things that constitute the world around us, any more than 'spirit' is a *thing* whose reality could be reduced to what is given to us in sense-experience.

One implication of Lagneau's point is that, paradoxical though it may sound, someone who denies God's existence in *that* sense is already closer to an adequate understanding of God's reality than those who take the opposite view. Weil, too, takes up this thought in *Gravity and Grace*, when she says that 'there are two atheisms of which one is a purification of the notion of God'.[53] Perhaps this also explains why a Christian writer like André Maurois could speak so highly of Alain's reflections on religious matters:

> Alain was most likely anticlerical, yet he was certainly religious. Few men have been able to speak more intelligently about Christianity. Indeed, he was the first man to reveal to me the greatness of Christian doctrine and induce me to accept so large a part of it.[54]

And Simone Weil? Even her earliest philosophical work already displays a fine religious sensibility, and a penetrating analysis of moral and aesthetic phenomena. One paper, in particular, should be mentioned here. It is entitled 'Le Beau et le Bien' (The Beautiful and the Good), and was written for Alain in 1926, when Weil was seventeen. In that paper, she is concerned with the kinds of considerations that would prompt us to say of an action that it is *beautiful*, and how, indeed, the notions of beauty and goodness are related to each other. In this connection, she uses a story about Alexander the Great as the background to her enquiry:

> Let us consider then a beautiful action. There is none more universally admired than that of Alexander who, suffering from thirst along with his whole army which he was leading across a desert, poured out on the ground a little water that a soldier had brought to him in a helmet. What are we thinking when we say that this action is beautiful?[55]

Weil knows that there will be readers who won't think that Alexander's action was beautiful at all – that pouring the water away was *useless*, for example, as Alexander was leading an army, and a thirsty leader is less likely to be efficient than one whose thirst has been quenched. Then again, there are those who will say that Alexander's spilling of the water *was* useful, in so far as it instilled courage in his men.[56] Weil rejects both of these readings, arguing instead that 'the utility of his action is in effect beside the point', and that, if we want to get to the heart of the matter, we must pay attention to other aspects of Alexander's action:

> Alexander, after a first movement that is purely mechanical, stands motionless while the soldier draws near. The army does not spring toward the water either, and it does not even look on it with greed; it directs its gaze to human signs, that is to say, it looks at its leader. Alexander, all the while the soldier was coming toward him, made no movement toward the water; when the soldier is close by, he finally takes the helmet, and stands motionless a moment. The army stands motionless too, its eyes fixed on him; and the universe is filled with the silence and the tension of expectation of these men. Suddenly, at the necessary instant, neither too soon nor too late, Alexander pours out the water; and the tension toward it is as it were released. No one, Alexander less than anyone, would have dared to foresee this astonishing action; but once the action is accomplished, there is no one who does not feel that it had to be like this.[57]

What makes Alexander's gesture a beautiful action, then, is that he remained *still* at the crucial moment, and that his subsequent pouring out of the water is part of a geometry of renunciation in which his own motives and those of his soldiers are perfectly aligned:

> And in effect the soldier who brings the water, and the army that looks at it, renounce the water too; they renounce it for Alexander; he renounces it for them; each man is, like the stones of a temple, at once end and means.[58]

In order to explore the implications of this insight further, Weil then goes on to change the circumstances of the original example and imagines an Alexander who is no longer surrounded by his army, but alone, perhaps stranded in a desert. Again, he is thirsty and comes upon some water. At the same time, he knows that his army is elsewhere in the desert, far away, and equally thirsty. Should he drink? A utilitarian observer would undoubtedly recommend that he does. Surely, it would be irrational not to drink when one is as thirsty as Alexander, and especially when there is no one else with a similarly strong claim to the water. Weil's response is clear: if Alexander drinks the water, there will be nothing beautiful in his action. It is the kind of action we would expect from a thirsty man, and nothing for which we would commend him. But if the Alexander in the desert is the same Alexander we encountered earlier, then he will *not* drink, even now that he is alone, because he knows that the act would separate him from his men even more than the spatial distance does. There is something saintly in this renewed renunciation, as the seventeen-year-old Weil is already well aware:

> The sacrifice consists in the acceptance of pain, in the refusal to obey the animal in oneself, and in the will to redeem suffering men by voluntary suffering. Every saint has poured out the water; every saint has refused all well-being that would separate him from the sufferings of men.[59]

When Weil wrote these lines, she was still many years away from making a similar choice to that which confronted Alexander in her early philosophical discussion of beauty and goodness, viz. to renounce her own well-being out of solidarity with her starving fellow – countrymen. As might have been expected, the general reaction to this gesture was one of incomprehension. On 31 August 1943, a week after her death, the Ashford *Tuesday Express* noted on page one:

French professor starves herself to death

It is both poignant and ironic that the response to Weil's death should be so similar to that of the imaginary utilitarians in her early essay on beauty and goodness.

4

Politics and the Needs of the Soul: Factory Work

Weil's decision to take a year's leave from her teaching duties, in order to experience at first hand the life of a factory worker, was motivated by practical as well as intellectual considerations. The practical motivation was a fervent desire to relieve the plight of the oppressed, whether they were to be found among political refugees, in the French colonies, or at a power press in a Parisian factory, and sprang from Weil's recognition that the duty of neighbourly love also demands the promotion of social justice. But the ubiquitous phenomena of self-alienation, social oppression, and degradation also had an intellectual dimension, in that these social ills had already occupied Weil's thinking long before her ordeal at the Alsthom and Renault factories in the period 1934–35, viz. as a concern to understand the causes of such social ills. It is one thing to promote liberty, social justice, and the need for revolutionary change on a leaflet drafted on a coffee table in the Latin Quarter, but quite another to have a clear idea of the nature of injustice and the root causes of oppression. For the latter, a certain amount of critical, theoretical reflection is indispensable:

> There is no contradiction whatever between this task of theoretical elucidation and the tasks set by the actual struggle; on the contrary, there is a correlation, since one cannot act without

knowing what one intends and what obstacles have to be overcome.[1]

On the other hand, Weil contends that a purely intellectual engagement with these obstacles is seriously deficient and must be both supplemented with, and deepened by, personal experience. This is why she tells her friend Albertine Thévenon, in a letter dated January 1935:

> Only when I think that the great Bolshevik leaders proposed to create a *free* working class and that doubtless none of them – certainly not Trotsky, and I don't think Lenin either – had ever set foot inside a factory, so that they hadn't the faintest idea of the real conditions which make servitude or freedom for the workers – well, politics appears to me a sinister farce.[2]

Weil's personal experiences of factory life are recorded in her autobiographical *Factory Journal*,[3] while her subsequent analysis of the wider issue of oppression can be found in the essay 'Reflections Concerning the Causes of Liberty and Social Oppression' (1936),[4] which will also be the focus of our present discussion. Echoing her earlier observation on Lenin and Trotsky, Weil begins by noting that most people's knowledge of the factory workers' plight is not immediate, but mediated through such organisations as the Front Populaire – an amalgam of Communist and other left-wing political activists, founded in 1935 – and that this detachment from 'the proletarian condition' can never yield more than a superficial grasp of the labourer's true predicament.

Even 'walks in the working-class quarters, glimpses of dark, miserable rooms, the houses, the streets, are no great help in understanding the life that people lead there',[5] because what matters are not merely the workers' living conditions as such, or their *external* circumstances, but their thoughts and feelings, and the character of their inner lives. Weil sees no contradiction in imagining a factory worker who, while enjoying more agreeable living conditions, would still feel alienated from his labour and thus 'uprooted', and she rejects as hopelessly naïve the claim that, if only the worker's general material circumstances were improved, the sense of oppression would be lifted along with it.

Weil's observation here anticipates her later discussion – in *The Need for Roots* – of essential human needs, whose satisfaction is required for individuals to feel truly at home in the culture they inhabit. One such need is that for equal consideration, independently of social status or material circumstances:

> Equality is a vital need of the human soul. It consists in a recognition, at once public, general, effective and genuinely expressed in institutions and customs, that the same amount of respect and consideration is due to every human being because this respect is due to the human being as such and is not a matter of degree.[6]

Another example of a vital human need would be to own property, both privately and collectively. It is rightly called a need of the *soul* because, as Weil explains, 'the soul feels isolated, lost, if it is not surrounded by objects which seem to it like an extension of the bodily members'.[7] Her point here is that there is a sense in which the objects we encounter in our environment, and with which we engage through our labour, for example, do not remain indifferent pieces of physical matter, but become extensions of ourselves and, by this very fact, invested with a *meaning* they would otherwise not have. If someone steals my stormproof umbrella, for example, he may not only be taking away something I need to shelter from the rain, but a *gift* from a dear friend, and thus something whose significance goes well beyond my appreciation of its material properties. The thief, of course, may not be aware of this, but it is clear that even the legal description of his act as the theft of an umbrella hardly captures what he has done to *me*. It is because Weil wants to highlight this meaning-relation between persons and things that she speaks of needs of the *soul*, and why she thinks it is 'desirable that the majority of people should own their house and a little piece of land round it, and, whenever not technically impossible, the tools of their trade',[8] and that, even at the collective level, 'each one feels he has a personal ownership in the public monuments, gardens, ceremonial pomp and circumstance'.[9]

However, while the satisfaction of the need for ownership or appropriation is vital, even workers who own an apartment and the tools of their trade will still feel uprooted if they are unemployed,[10] for example, or if the nature of their work or their general working environment is experienced as alienating and oppressive. Thus, in a clear allusion to Karl Marx's claim that an essential ingredient in the liberation of the proletariat from the fetters of capitalist oppression must be the abolition of private property in the major means of production, Weil plausibly retorts that 'the abolition of private property would be far from sufficient in itself to prevent work in the mines and in the factories from continuing to weigh as a servitude on those who are subjected to it'.[11]

Weil realised soon after entering the factory that the most elementary difficulty consisted in understanding and describing what the workers were going through, and that neither an outsider nor the workers themselves were, in fact, able to articulate the reasons for their suffering. She admits that a talented and highly imaginative writer like Jules Romain (1885–1972) may have produced an interesting chapter on factory life in his novel cycle *Les Hommes de bonne volonté* (*Men of Good Will*), 'but that kind of thing does not cut very deep',[12] nor can we expect it to. As for the workers themselves, who might have been thought to be the best source of illumination, Weil finds that they 'do not find it easy to write, speak, or even reflect on such a subject, for the first effect of suffering is the attempt of thought to *escape*. It refuses to confront the adversity that wounds it.'[13] The psychological mechanisms of repression, denial, and escape make sober and lucid reflection difficult, even in veteran workers for whom the ordeal is now a thing of the past, and when they talk about it at all, they tend to express themselves in the jargon coined by those who are *not* workmen, such as political functionaries and intellectuals. Thus, the problem of *understanding* the predicament of the factory worker involves a peculiar paradox: an outsider and impartial spectator does not know what factory work is really like, and those who witness it from the inside are unable to put their experiences into words.

Weil herself does not pursue the matter further, but it is tempting to think now that the depth missing from Jules Romain's depiction of factory life could easily be supplied by *anyone* (an investigative journalist, perhaps?) with first-hand experience of factory work. The fact that this conclusion does not follow, however, becomes clear when we remind ourselves that the experience of suffering itself is no guarantee of lucidity, as Hans Castorp discovered to his great dismay on visiting the *moribundi* in their last hour; far from detecting in their demeanour a certain lucidity and depth, he found only frivolity and superficiality. What a genuine understanding of the workers' plight requires, then, is not merely the shared experience of their tasks and movements, but acute powers of observation, intellectual independence, and a conceptual inventory that enables one to articulate one's experiences in a way that avoids the jargon employed by outside political activists and factory workers alike.

Weil herself, fortunate to possess all these attributes to a very high degree, is in no doubt that the workers' condition is one of *servitude*, manifested in the following phenomena: first, there is the time-clock, together with the rule that, within the confines of factory life, *chance* does not exist:

> In a man's work-day it is the first onslaught of a regimen whose brutality dominates a life spent among machines: the rule that chance has no place, no 'freedom of the city', in a factory. Chance exists there, of course, as it does anywhere else, but it is not recognised.[14]

Workers are subjected to blindly obeying orders that appear whimsical and arbitrary, and when they ask for reasons and explanations, they are callously rebuffed with the formula 'Never mind the reasons!', and the equally unenlightening insistence that the work *must* go on.[15] A great deal of needless suffering is created in this way, from the strict obligation to start work at *exactly* 8 a.m., rather than 8.05 a.m. or 8.10 a.m., say, to the prideful condescension displayed by superiors, to contradictory orders and arbitrary changes of work assignments. Weil is struck by the irony of such conduct, as it merely hinders, rather than enhances, the productivity in' whose name it is ostensibly engaged. And the workers themselves? Knowing that there would be no point in complaining, indeed that 'to speak of such things ... would be an invitation to humiliation',[16] they say nothing and keep their anger inside.

What makes this response an instance of *uprootedness*, for Weil, is that the workers' natural and instinctive reactions of indignation are stifled and suppressed, leading to inertia and passivity. Under normal circumstances, they *would* complain about such treatment, but here they don't, with the result that ordinary responses to injustice are gradually eroded. Weil expresses the point well when she says,

> The fact that he would like to forget, that he cannot feel at home in the plant, that he has no freedom of movement there, that he is an alien given admittance only in his capacity as intermediary between machines and the things to be machined, all this eats into body and soul; and flesh and thought shrink back. It is as though someone were repeating in his ear at every passing moment and with all possibility of reply excluded: 'Here, you are

nothing. You simply do not count. You are here to obey, to accept everything, to keep your mouth shut.'[17]

In the course of time, as the worker's subjugation and humiliation continues, he 'comes to acquiesce deep down that he counts for nothing', and to attach more importance to the quantifiable reality of money than to the diffuse and inexpressible feelings he has while at work.[18] At this point, Weil contrasts the work routine of a factory worker with that of a traditional artisan, to highlight the degree of *control* and *liberty* in the execution of the latter's tasks:

The modest artisan who possesses a machine shop and who knows that within a fortnight he must have ready so many braces and bits, so many faucets, or so many connecting rods, is not precisely free to do as he pleases with his time either, but at least, once an order is accepted, he may determine in advance the employment he will give his days and hours.[19]

What distinguishes the artisan's working conditions from that of the factory labourer is that he can 'mentally embrace the immediate future' and thereby also 'possess' it, as it were, whereas the factory worker 'must be ready at any moment to take an order. Like an inert object that anyone may move about at will.'[20] According to Weil, such treatment is not only undignified but, in spite of popular slogans about the 'progress' of the modern age, testimony to a condition which even our allegedly more 'primitive' ancestors did not have to endure:

The constraint is in certain cases incomparably more brutal today than it has ever been. However tied and bound a primitive man was to routine and blind gropings, he could at least try to think things out, to combine and innovate at his own risk, a liberty which is absolutely denied to a worker engaged in a production line.[21]

The conditions of factory life induce a kind of schizophrenia: on the one hand, the worker is forced to live by the rule that, inside the factory, there is no such thing as chance, even though he *knows* this to be false; on the other hand, that very same rule is reduced *ad absurdum* by the unpredictable will of his boss, who issues unjust orders and arbitrarily changes the worker's assignment from one moment to the next. In addition, the worker is condemned to 'visualising monotonous desert regions of experience that thought has no way of exploring'.[22]

A monotonous work routine, Weil notes in *The Need for Roots*, 'brings with it disgust, and time hangs with an almost intolerable heaviness'.[23] The only way for the worker to sidestep it, however, is to imagine an unexpected order, but then he also realises that such an order would involve further humiliation, so his thought 'draws back from the future' and the tedium of his work presses on his soul unrelieved.[24] Paradoxically, the very unpredictability that, under normal circumstances, would be a welcome relief of monotony, in the factory setting becomes a major source of apprehension – e.g. a fear of what the foreman might say, or of a cut in earnings for not working fast enough, etc. – coupled with a sense of impotence, dependency, and unworthiness:

> What makes matters worse is the permanent possibility of an accident: Nothing is worse than a mixture of monotony and accident. They are mutually aggravating, at least when accident is bound up with anxiety. In a factory, accident *is* a source of anxiety, for the very reason that accident has no status there.[25]

Weil's point here is that the worker's fear of an accident is not reducible to the fear that he might be physically harmed, though he is, of course, worried about that as well. The likely reaction of his superiors considerably adds to his anxiety, as he knows that he would be blamed for slowing down production, and that his accident would be regarded as a nuisance, rather than as an occasion for compassionate care. Everything is subordinated to the abstract *diktat* of the productive process, and the foreman's indignant reaction to 'accidents' is symptomatic of a more general refusal to embrace the truth: in theory, there is no shortage of supplies, a machine never stalls, any more than a toolbox goes missing or the foreman keeps changing his mind, but in reality the opposite is true. 'The need of truth', however, 'is more sacred than any other need', Weil notes in *The Need for Roots*,[26] and a major aspect of the factory worker's degradation consists precisely in the denial of that need.

The Czech writer and political dissident Vaclav Havel (1936–) who, after the fall of Communism, became president of Czechoslovakia and later president of the Czech Republic, has provided an excellent elaboration on this topic in his essay 'The Power of the Powerless'.[27] It is part of a detailed and subtle analysis of life under a Communist regime, and well worth reading alongside Weil's own reflections on the subject.[28] Using the example of a greengrocer who displays in his window the slogan 'Workers of the world, unite!', Havel asks: 'Why does he do it? What is he trying to communicate to the world? Is he genuinely enthusiastic about the idea of unity among the workers of the world?'[29] Havel's sober response, reflective of the equally sobering reality behind the façade of Communist propaganda, is that, in putting up the slogan, the greengrocer is not expressing his real opinions at all. As Havel observes:

> That poster was delivered to our greengrocer from the enterprise headquarters along with the onions and carrots. He put them all into the window simply because it has been done that way for years, because everyone does it, and because that is the way it has to be. If he were to refuse, there could be trouble. He could be reproached for not having the proper 'decoration' in his window; someone might even accuse him of disloyalty. He does it because these things must be done if one is to get along in life. It is one of the thousands of details that guarantee him a relatively tranquil life 'in harmony with society', as they say.[30]

Now imagine that the greengrocer had displayed in his window the sign 'I am afraid and therefore unquestioningly obedient'. It would have expressed the truth but, as Havel rightly notes, 'the greengrocer would be embarrassed and ashamed to put such an unequivocal statement of his own degradation in the shop window, and quite naturally so, for he is a human being and thus has a sense of his own dignity'.[31] Instead, he displays the party-political slogan and behaves *as if* he believed in it, so as to get on with life. The only problem, however, is that he is now living *within a lie*.[32] Similarly with the workers in Weil's factory: fully aware that, if they question any of the foreman's pronouncements, the bill won't be long in coming, they are forced to live within a lie as well and, as a consequence, suffer even more from spiritual exhaustion than they do from physical fatigue.

And the worker's relation to his co-workers? Factory life has its moments of camaraderie, of course, but these are rare and insufficient to compensate for the indifference with which his superiors, in particular, react to his accomplishments. 'Such indifference', Weil says, 'is a privation of that human warmth which will always be in some degree necessary',[33] though its evaporation is not at all surprising in an atmosphere where the end-products of labour count for everything and the details of their genesis are considered unimportant. Note that Weil's observation about the worker's plight also carries implications for our own attitude towards the fruits of his labour. Should we not be interested in their *history* as well, in the story of how they were made? A connoisseur of fine coffee, for example, rarely wonders whether the worker who picked the beans may have fainted in the heat of the sun, been bullied by a foreman, or forced to live in poverty through exploitation. The example is also worth contemplating because it shows something about how the *ethical* dimensions of the labour process tend to be concealed from our awareness. In this context, Weil speaks of a perverse inversion of *means* and *ends*, in which men are reduced to things, and things come to play the role of men:

> The parts circulate with labels bearing their name, material, and degree of elaboration; one could almost believe that they are the persons, and the workers the interchangeable parts. The parts have their identity card tantamount to a description of civil condition; and when it is necessary, as in certain large factories, to show one's card with the photograph bearing, convict-like, a number on the breast, the symbolic contrast becomes poignant.[34]

If the worker wants to complete his tasks, he needs a *motive* to do so, and the only one that propels him relentlessly on is 'the fear of being "bawled out" or fired, or the eagerness to fatten one's pay envelope, and, in some cases, an interest in speed records'.[35] In time, this (low) motive becomes obsessive and 'an almost irresistible force, comparable to that of gravity', gradually turns the worker into a mirror image of the same brutality that fuels the factory system itself. He no longer notices the fellow-worker beside him, and blindly plays his part in a mechanised routine whose details he knows nothing about. He becomes a cog in a chain of operations in which every worker serves as a means for handling and passing on the parts he has received from his predecessor, without any *understanding* of the way in which the various stages in the productive process are connected, or of what contribution he, in particular, is making to it.

As Marx had already noted in his detailed analysis of capitalist oppression, the division between manual and intellectual labour is itself a major source of degradation, as it wilfully ignores the basic human need to engage with the world reflectively and with understanding. Hence Weil's programmatic comment that

We want to give to manual labour that dignity which belongs to it of right, by giving the workman the full understanding of technical processes instead of a mere mechanical training; and to provide the understanding with its proper object, by placing it in contact with the world through the medium of labour.[36]

Weil's point could also be expressed in Kantian terms: given that all human beings are invested with an intrinsic and inviolable dignity – in virtue of which they are *ends in themselves*, rather than simply *means* to this or that end – and that their needs are both physical and intellectual, it follows that their dignity is being seriously violated if these needs are deliberately ignored. And is it not paradoxical that the very workers who are indispensable to the productive process also count for nothing?[37] Weil illustrates their intellectual predicament with an excellent analogy:

The number 2 thought of by one man cannot be added to the number 2 thought of by another man so as to make up the number 4; similarly, the idea that one of the cooperators has of the partial work he is carrying out cannot be combined with the idea that each of the others has of his respective task so as to form a coherent piece of work.[38]

What is required, therefore, is a radical transformation, not merely of the general conditions under which the factory worker must earn his living, but of the *incentives* that prompt him to work: 'acquisitiveness and the fear of dismissal', for instance, 'must cease to be the main motives', and should be replaced with 'the feeling of an end to be accomplished and a job to be done.'[39] But Weil has further suggestions about how the situation of the factory worker might be improved: (1) workers should be given an opportunity to explore the plant at which they are employed;[40] (2) the products of their labour must be seen to satisfy some concrete social need or other; (3) purely repetitive and simple movements in the productive process should be transferred to a machine; (4) proper attention must be given to the importance of time and rhythm in structuring the worker's tasks;[41] (5) the workers should have advance knowledge of what is expected of them, and be given a say in the chronology of their assignments.[42] In addition, school education 'must be conceived in an entirely new way' as well, so 'that it may shape men capable of understanding the total aspects of the work in which they will be taking part'.[43]

The question of how men should engage with the world through labour is thus shown to be connected with far wider issues than pay, the representation of workers' rights, the length of the working day, or the quality of the food served in factory canteens, and it is a fine testimony to Weil's *attention* to these wider issues that, in spite of her personal ordeals, she thought of them. And while the language she uses in her description of the workers' plight is not religious, except when she sees in man's natural need 'to pause on having finished something, if only for an instant, in order to contemplate his handiwork' a reflection of God's pause in the Genesis story,[44] her references to human dignity are strongly reminiscent of Kant's ethical ideals, and could be regarded as a secular analogue of the thought that man is created in God's image, and therefore free, equal, and deserving of his neighbour's love.

Even after her time in the factory, Weil continued to explore the above issues in greater detail, most notably in a series of essays gathered in *Oppression and Liberty*, and of course she also asked herself whether the workers' plight could be adequately remedied by the kind of proletarian revolution envisaged and predicted by Marx. Weil's critical engagement with Marx, Marxism and the idea of revolutionary change can also be found in that collection, and is profitably followed up in Lawrence A. Blum and Victor J. Seidler's superb discussion in *A Truer Liberty: Simone Weil and Marxism*. I shall not pursue the issue here, save to note that, in spite of her admiration for Marx's insights into the causes of oppression, alienation, and exploitation, and much though she applauds his incisive criticisms of the capitalist mode of production, Weil strongly rejects the claim that the course of human history inevitably leads to the establishment of a Communist world order in which the ills of oppression have finally been eliminated. But her reservations are perhaps best illustrated with an analogy. In *Portraits from Memory*, the philosopher Bertrand Russell tells us that, not long after he had discovered the 'dazzling' and 'delicious' world of mathematical demonstrations, he 'hoped that in time there would be a mathematics of human behaviour as precise as the mathematics of machines' – 'I hoped this', he says, 'because I liked demonstrations.'[45]

Russell's idea of a 'mathematics of human behaviour' bears a striking resemblance to the utopian ideals of Herr Settembrini, in Chapter 5 ('Encyclopaedic') of Thomas Mann's *Magic Mountain*, and is likely to elicit just as much scepticism. In the course of a lengthy discussion with Hans Castorp, the humanist Settembrini reports on the work of the 'League for the Organisation of Pro-gress', whose end is the total and final elimination of all human suffering. A major step in this direction will be the publication of a comprehensive socio-pathology of pain and affliction, which the ecstatic Settembrini describes as follows:

> It will be issued in some twenty folio volumes, treating every species of human suffering, from the most personal and intimate to the great collective struggles arising from the conflicting interests of classes and nations; it will, in short, exhibit the chemical elements whose combination in various proportions results in all the ills to which our common flesh is heir. ... Famous European specialists, physicians, psychologists, and economists will share in the composition of this encyclopaedia of suffering, and the general editorial bureau at Lugano will act as the reservoir to collect all the articles which shall flow into it.[46]

The philanthropic motivation behind the League's project is admirable enough and would certainly be endorsed by Weil herself. What is not so admirable, however, is the prideful and overly self-confident tone – what the Greeks called *hubris* – in which that project is presented; the naïve assumption that, if only the right sort of 'League' is established to take care of human needs, many of the contingencies to which our lives are currently prone will be effi-ciently eliminated, so that there will be no further 'accidents' in terms of unforeseen physical or psychological affliction; and the altogether abstract and indeterminate notion of progress that underlies it.

What is required instead, so Weil would argue, is the kind of reflection she herself provides in *The Need for Roots*, and it is to this that readers must turn if they want to get a better understanding of man's essential needs and how these are to be met within the con-text of social life, in particular. The parallels between Russell's and Settembrini's naïveté on the one hand, and Marx's confidence in the advent of the Communist state on the other, are easy to see, and it should not come as a surprise to Weil's readers that her final verdict on Marx's utopia is rather more sobering than he and his followers would have liked:

> Humanity has always placed in God its hope of quenching its thirst for justice. Once God no longer inhabited men's souls, that hope had either to be discarded or to be placed in matter. Man

cannot bear to be alone in willing the good. He needs an all-powerful ally. If this ally is not spirit, it will be matter. It is simply a case of two different expressions of the same fundamental thought. But the second expression is defective. It is a badly constructed religion. But it is a religion. There is, therefore, nothing surprising in the fact that Marxism has always possessed a religious character. It has a great many things in common with the forms of religious life most bitterly attacked by Marx, especially in having frequently been used, to quote Marx's own formula, as the opium of the people. But it is a religion devoid of mystique, in the true sense of the word.[47]

5

Religious Reflection (1): God, the Christian Inspiration, and the Incarnation

Introduction

As we have seen, Simone Weil's insights into the human condition are the result of a complex interplay between disinterested philosophical contemplation on the one hand and personal experience on the other, and the authority with which she can speak on such issues as school education, the spiritual value of mathematics, the nature of beauty and goodness, or the plight of the wage-labourer derives precisely from this dynamic dialectic. For her, a reflective engagement with the world is not only an intellectual but an ethical requirement, for it acknowledges not only Kant's reminder that ideas disconnected from experience are empty,[1] but Socrates' exhortation that the unexamined life is not worth living, and the recognition that personal integrity, authenticity, and a certain kind of unity between thought and action are intimately interwoven.

Weil is, of course, aware that these reminders describe only the *formal* conditions of an authentic life, to which an agnostic humanist might assent just as readily as a devout religious believer, a humanitarian atheist, or a philanthropic pessimist.[2] Indeed, even the life of a heinous criminal could exhibit a perfect congruence of thought and action, revealing the agent to be authentically himself in every criminal act he performs. He may have a reputation for always meaning what he says, and for unfailingly acting on his intentions, and of course this is precisely what would make him the dangerous individual that he is.

What still needs to be addressed, therefore, is the question of *content* – of what, in Weil's view, makes a life both authentic in the sense just described, and authentically *Christian*. Closely connected with this question is the issue of the contrast, so firmly entrenched in the minds of many believers and atheists alike, between 'pagan' or 'secular' attitudes, on the one hand, and Christian or religious perspectives on life, on the other. And doesn't this contrast itself rest on the assumption that the concepts of the secular and the religious have clear and mutually exclusive boundaries? If that assumption turned out to be false, then what would this mean for religious belief more generally, and for our understanding of the Christian faith, in particular? A more open construal of the dichotomies secular/religious, pagan/Christian, and Christian/non-Christian would undoubtedly affect the character of the relation between these seemingly incompatible perspectives in fundamental ways, both theoretically and practically.

Simone Weil, ever mindful of the ways in which such distinctions have been employed throughout the history of Christianity to condemn, excommunicate, torture, and even kill those who were unfortunate enough to find themselves on the wrong side of the divide, does not shy away from these questions, and a large part of her writing between 1937 and 1943 is an attempt to grapple with them. For her, this enquiry is of crucial importance: first, for the self-understanding of religious believers who call themselves Christians; and second, for the history of the Church to which they have pledged their allegiance. Both the individual and the institution share a common past to which they are answerable through retrospective evaluation and assessment, and so one can ask, for example, whether the Christian Church has been genuinely faithful to its divine mission, and what its relation should be to people of other faiths or none. It is because these questions force us to reflect on the very nature of the Christian faith that Weil raises them. She wants to know what it means to call oneself a Christian, and while the question also expresses a deeply *personal* need, viz. to know where she herself stands in relation to the Christian ideal, it is really addressed to *anyone* whose life is seriously oriented towards a certain conception of love, including those who do not regard themselves as Christians at all.

Once again, the character of Weil's reflections on Christianity, and the conclusions she eventually draws from them, are best understood against the background of her autobiographical remarks. Here, her *Spiritual Autobiography* of 1942 – already mentioned in Chapter 2 – is a good starting point, also because it provides us with a helpful synopsis of the various issues that were to occupy her during the last five years of her life. We shall use it as a framework for expounding the religious reflection of her later years, and continue to draw on her other writings for further elucidation. Before doing so, however, it is worth recalling what Gustave Thibon, the earliest editor of Weil's writings, tells us about the interpretative difficulties and temptations he faced when he first encountered her work. As he notes in his introduction to *Gravity and Grace*,

> a Catholic who has to assess the thought of a non-Catholic has difficulty in avoiding two opposite extremes. The first consists of applying the principles of speculative theology to the thought in question and mercilessly condemning everything which, seen from outside, does not appear to be strictly orthodox. ... The second danger consists of trying at whatever cost to bend the thought one is studying into conformity with Catholic truth.[3]

For Gustave Thibon, the most profitable approach to Weil's writings is not to come 'armed with a sort of Baedeker of divine things' and to pronounce judgement on the orthodoxy of her thoughts, but to study her work in a charitable spirit, 'in order to find nourishment for [one's] spiritual life'.[4] This exhortation is not only fair, but all the more pertinent given the fragmentary nature of Weil's reflections on religion, especially in the *Notebooks*, which it is tempting to 'tidy up' into a coherent and logically consistent account of the nature of the spiritual life. The temptation, though natural, should be strongly resisted. Weil does not write as a theologian or philosophical system-builder, let alone as a Catholic catechist or neo-Kantian idealist, but, as Thibon aptly puts it, 'a heroic explorer' of Christian spirituality in its diverse manifestations.[5] To regard her work as an exploration will not, of course, eliminate the tensions which undoubtedly exist between her own conception of the Christian faith and that of her readers, but it should guard them against taking her views in too dogmatic a spirit, and open up possibilities of illumination that would otherwise have eluded them.

Weil's spiritual journey

At first sight, Weil's spiritual development presents a straightforward trajectory from a certain kind of philosophically-enlightened agnosticism, through a phase of fervent, if ultimately disillusioned, political activism, to an intensely personal and ineffable experience of Christ's love, as a consequence of which she abandons her earlier agnosticism and becomes a devout proponent of the Christian faith. That this would be a crude and superficial genealogy of Weil's spiritual journey, however, should already be evident from what has been said about the character of her adolescent crisis, the deeply religious overtones of her earliest reflections on beauty and goodness, the transcendental orientation of the philosophers who most influenced her thinking, her appreciation of mythology and folklore as transcultural expressions of value, and her philosophical reflections on the nature of existence and perception. Weil's spiritual self-assessment of 1942 rather suggests that the movement of her thought is not so much from disbelief to faith in Christ and the God of the New Testament, but a progressive deepening of an attitude whose character remains fundamentally unchanged, no matter what aspect of her life is singled out for close inspection.

What she is inviting us to consider, once we have acquired an overview of her central, spiritual concerns, is whether there would be anything idolatrous in calling the general orientation of her life 'Christian'. If not, then that verdict must also carry implications for the Church's understanding of the spiritual condition of all those who share that orientation. So how does she herself describe the evolution of her thought, and what conclusions did her experiences and reflections lead her to embrace?

Searching for God

Contrary to a common way of speaking, Weil is reluctant to characterise her spiritual journey as a 'search for God' – an expression that seems to her not only misleading, but false:

> I may say that never at any moment in my life have I 'sought for God'. For this reason, which is probably too subjective, I do not like this expression and it strikes me as false. As soon as I

reached adolescence, I saw the problem of God as a problem the data of which could not be obtained here below, and I decided that the only way of being sure not to reach a wrong conclusion, which seemed to me the greatest possible evil, was to leave it alone. So I left it alone. I neither affirmed nor denied anything.[6]

It is not immediately clear why Weil rejects the expression 'I was searching for God' as false, since one can imagine contexts in which this would be a perfectly intelligible and appropriate thing to say. On the other hand, her subsequent remark about God's existence and the relation between the 'data' available to us 'here below' suggests that her reservations have to do with the peculiar nature of religious as opposed to other kinds of belief, and with the function and limitations of the human intellect. Let us take these points in turn and begin by considering the following beliefs:

(a) The Social Democrats will win the next election.
(b) There is intelligent extraterrestrial life.
(c) Hölderlin was *not* mad.
(d) Suicide is wrong.
(e) Mozart was a sublime composer.
(f) God exists.

Now, it is clear that (a)–(c) fall into a different category from (d)–(f). While the former may elicit a request for reasons in the form of supporting evidence, the latter typically do not. I might, for instance, justify (a) by citing the findings of reliable opinion polls, support (b) with a scholarly article I've read in *Astronomer's Weekly*, and back up (c) by reference to Pierre Bertaux's ground-breaking study of Hölderlin, which suggests to me that, contrary to common opinion, much of the German poet's strange conduct in the latter period of his life is explicable without recourse to the notion of mental illness.[7] Moreover, it would be perfectly legitimate to speak of (a)–(c) as *hypotheses* awaiting confirmation, or as beliefs whose truth was more or less *probable*, depending on the strength of the available evidential support.

Another feature of (a)–(c) is that they themselves need not necessarily manifest in ways that are publicly observable. There *may* be such manifestations, of course – for example, when belief in (a) prompts someone to transfer his savings to a foreign bank because he knows that the Social Democrats will immediately increase capital gains tax after the election, and he does not want to pay such a tax. In this case, belief in (a) could be said to be a sufficient condition for his taking the said measures. Conversely, if our prudent investor knew that there were substantial legal and other risks involved in transferring his money abroad, the belief in (a) might be a necessary but not a sufficient condition of his carrying out the proposed transaction. Then again, the agent might be wholly indifferent, not only to taxation, but to the outcome of the forthcoming elections, in which case his belief in (a) would not even be a necessary condition of his transfers abroad. It does not follow from this, however, that he does not subscribe to (a). All that follows is that (a) does not affect him but leaves him cold, as it were.

Thus, what shows whether an agent believes in the forthcoming victory of the Social Democrats may be no more than a thought to that effect – entertained in the light of newspaper reports, perhaps – or the corresponding assertion, when explicitly asked about the matter. There is, in any event, nothing odd about believing something without being particularly affected by it, and (a)–(c) are illustrations of this. A cultural philistine with no interest whatever in Hölderlin's poetry might yet be curious to know whether a retrospective re-evaluation of a poet's mental condition could be convincingly put forward, and he might come to embrace (c) as a consequence of Bertaux's study, perhaps even incorporate it – purely for entertainment purposes – into his dinner table conversations. Pierre Bertaux himself, on the other hand, has no doubt been deeply affected by his findings, not least because of his thorough familiarity with, and great love of, Hölderlin's work, which now appears in a new light. Unlike the philistine, Bertaux does not regard (c) merely as a curious fact, but as a truth with profound consequences for his own understanding of Hölderlin's poetry, of the distinction between madness and sanity, and of the explanatory potential of painstaking biographical research.

Similar things could be said about (b), depending on whether the agent was merely a collector of statistical curiosities, or a writer like Erich von Däniken, whose life's work revolves around (b) and expresses itself in his numerous books and public lectures, no less than in his extensive travels. The general point behind these observations is that there are circumstances where (a)–(c) are manifested at best verbally, and where we would find this neither surprising nor shocking. There is a sense, in other words, in which indifference to the truth of (a)–(c) would be quite an intelligible reaction. This is not so in the case of (d)–(f), however, at least not if the latter are professed with any degree of seriousness.

If one believes that suicide is wrong, that Mozart was a sublime composer, or that there is a God, one will hardly register with indifference the suicide of Heinrich von Kleist, the claim that Mozart was a second-rate musical dilettante, or Nietzsche's declaration that God is dead. This comes out in the way that denials of (d)–(f) would typically be characterised, viz. as morally outrageous, insulting, and blasphemous, respectively.

As the above discussion has shown, such vocabulary is *not* naturally applicable to the negations of (a)–(c). There would be nothing morally reprehensible or blasphemous about either believing or disbelieving in an imminent electoral victory of the Social Democrats, intelligent life in the universe, or Hölderlin's alleged madness, since these beliefs are not evaluated in terms of moral or religious categories, but in terms of evidential support, probable truth, empirical confirmation, etc. Indeed, if (a)–(c) *are* well supported by empirical evidence, or have been shown to be either true or probably true, it would be odd to reject them on the grounds of moral or religious impropriety. With the value judgements expressed in (d)–(f), on the other hand, questions about their evidential support or probability do not arise, not because these judgements are not answerable to a substantive criterion of truth, but because their respective objects – the moral status of suicide, musical greatness, God – have a different grammar from those determining the sense of (a)–(c).

It might be objected that this account of (d)–(f) is not quite accurate, since something *could* be said in support of (d)–(f). Elaborating on his claim that suicide is wrong, for example, someone might say – as Socrates does in the *Phaedo* – that (d') life is a gift, or that (d″) it would be an act of cowardice to take one's life. But this objection is misguided. For if Socrates' elaborations are taken to be supporting reasons for (d), one would expect these to put (d) on firmer ground than it would be without them, similarly to the way in which astrophysical data would support (b), or Pierre Bertaux's collation of biographical data would reinforce (c).

It is clear, however, that neither of Socrates' elaborations has this effect, since the same question would then arise with regard to (d') and (d″): what reason is there for thinking that life is a gift, or that suicide is a cowardly act? Some, like Schopenhauer, consider life a punishment; others, a gift. Some think that suicide is cowardly; others, that it is the most perfect expression of human freedom. There is no *evidence*, however, that would support one view more strongly than the other, not because the right evidence has not yet come to light, but because it is not even clear what would *count* as evidence here.

One reason for rejecting talk of evidence in connection with (d)–(f) is that they seem to be *personal* in a way that (a)–(c) are not. If a former atheist were to tell me that he had converted to Catholicism and now believed in God, for example, I would not take him to be suggesting that anyone who carefully considered the evidence, or followed some procedure P, was bound to believe in God as well. His profession of belief would be a personal confession concerning a radical transformation in his intellectual, emotional, and spiritual orientation. As Wittgenstein says in *Zettel*: ' "You can't hear God speak to someone else, you can hear him only if you are being addressed". That is a grammatical remark.'[8] Belief or faith in God appears to be somewhat analogous to moral insight or aesthetic appreciation, in that it neither springs from, nor requires, *external* justifications in the form of evidential support or statistical probabilities.

Just as someone to whom classical music means nothing is unlikely to appreciate Rubinstein's performance of Chopin's *Nocturnes*, simply by being told about the Polish musical tradition, the Irish composer John Field, etc., so an unbeliever is unlikely to 'hear' God's voice simply by overhearing a conversation between two Catholics. He could make little of the language, pictures, symbols, and gestures that characterise the believer's life, since he does not see his own life in that way, nor is there a method whose application guarantees that he will come to do so. It is in this sense, too, that one can hear God only if one is being addressed.

Of course, if our unbeliever overheard a conversation between two Jehovah's Witnesses assuring each other of the 'historical accuracy' of the Scriptures and the 'cumulative evidence' of their truth, he might well come to believe that there was a God. But then, wouldn't his belief be analogous to (b), to which talk of evidence and justification *is* relevant, and wouldn't the object of his belief then have the grammatical status of the sorts of object that determine the sense of (a)–(c)? In that case, it looks as if he might just as well have arrived at his belief by listening to a conversation between two particle physicists who, wondering whether God might not be the ultimate explanation behind the Big Bang, end up concluding 'God exists!' However, as the German theologian Armin Kreiner has rightly noted, 'to know that there is a God means nothing as long as you do not know what "God" means,'[9] so what kind of god are we talking about? Is it

[the] God of Abraham, Isaac and Jacob or the God of Spinoza and Einstein? The God of the Bible or the Qur'an or the Bhagavadgita or maybe one of the ancient Greek or Roman gods or one of the Indian *devas* or Japanese *kamp*? Would you know whether there is someone out there listening to your prayers and laments, someone who cares about you? Would you know whether there is someone to deliver you from evil, sin and death?[10]

The answer is, of course, 'no', and it is difficult to see how we *could* come to know such things in the absence of the wider conceptual and linguistic frameworks in which belief in God is normally embedded. According to the Nicene Creed, for example, to believe in God is also to believe in Jesus Christ, the only Son of God; in the Holy Spirit, 'who proceeds from the Father and the Son' and who 'has spoken through the prophets'; in the holy, catholic, and apostolic Church; in the forgiveness of sins, and in the resurrection of the dead.

If the adolescent Simone Weil took little interest in speculative disputes about God's existence, it was not because she was hastily dismissive of that venerable tradition of medieval natural theology – epitomised in such thinkers as the Muslim theologian Al-Ghazali and the Franciscan friar St Bonaventure – and the arguments it advanced in support of the belief that there is a God. While it is true that she thought 'the problem of God' to be irresolvable by means of such arguments, and that any deliberate 'search' for God – either intellectually, or through certain sorts of experience – was unlikely to succeed, she also realised that there was a world of difference between intellectual assent to an argument for God's existence, and believing in the living God of the New Testament. As Rush Rhees puts it:

Suppose you had to explain to someone who had no idea at all of religion or of what a belief in God was. Could you do it in this way? – By proving to him that there must be a first cause – a Something – and that this Something is more powerful (whatever this means) than anything else: so that you would not have been conceived or born at all but for the operation of Something, and Something might wipe out the existence of everything at any time? Would this give him any sense of the wonder and glory of God? Would he not be justified if he answered, 'What a horrible idea! Like a Frankenstein without limits, so that you cannot escape it. The most ghastly nightmare!'[11]

As we saw in Chapter 3, Kant's distinction between noumena and phenomena carries important implications for our understanding of God and the transcendent, including the recognition that God must not be viewed as a phenomenon among phenomena, but as the transcendental ground – to speak of 'cause' would be inappropriate here, as Kant takes the category of causality to apply only to the phenomenal realm – and sustainer of the world. It is interesting to note that, when Weil expresses the same insight in *Gravity and Grace*, she does so in an idiom that deliberately eschews the often technical and spiritually antiseptic terminology of Kant's *Critique of Pure Reason*. 'God', she tells us, 'can only be present in creation under the form of absence', and consequently the believer's task is best described in terms of a paradox:

> Nothing which exists is absolutely worthy of love. We must therefore love that which does not exist. This non-existent object of love is not a fiction, however, for our fictions cannot be any more worthy of love than we are ourselves, and we are not worthy of it.[12]

Weil's repeated emphasis on the radical difference between God and his creation is reminiscent of the considerably more elaborate doctrine of divine simplicity advanced by such medieval theologians as Anselm of Canterbury and Thomas Aquinas.[13] Unlike all earthly creatures, God is 'simple' in that he is not a member of *any* class, so he is also *unique* in a way that his creatures are not. This is why, as Brian Davies observes,

> [We] cannot, for example, suppose that God is part of the world of space and time. Nor can we suppose him subject to the limitations and changes which affect things spatial and temporal. So it will be nonsense to speak of God as literally being *here* as opposed to *there*, or as literally being *now* as opposed to *then*. And it will be nonsense to speak of God as literally being first *like this* and then *like that*. It will be nonsense to say that divinity is something passing through successive states. And it will be even more nonsense to think of God as changing because other things have an effect on him. So it will be wrong to say that creatures can do something to modify God somehow.[14]

It is worth noting that, insofar as Weil agrees with this conception of the divine – and the textual evidence certainly suggests that she does – she would also find herself in fundamental disagreement with contemporary 'process theologians', according to whom God is not only a conscious agent, but a being who learns and changes over time. If Weil had lived to read the controversial §§198–231 of the new Catholic catechism, in which the ancient doctrine of divine simplicity is vigorously upheld over alternative construals, she would no doubt have greeted it with much applause. As for Weil's suggestion that the only thing worthy of unconditional love is that which does not 'exist', viz. God, this is not intended to qualify the commandment of neighbourly love, but to draw attention to the supremacy of God's will over the requirements of worldly attachment, whether to people or things. This thought is only a starting point for further reflection on the relation between love and its objects, however, and what Weil would like us to understand is that paradoxes of this kind – 'To love God is to love that which does not exist' – are an essential part of religious reflection, and that, if these are to provide spiritual nourishment, we must resist the temptation to explain or dissolve them: 'The contemplation of these absurdities draws one upwards, if they are contemplated *as absurd* (they must not then be defended).'[15]

Viewed from a certain angle, belief in God may appear irrational or absurd, and the believer as tragicomic figure who seems to be staking his whole life on something for whose existence there isn't the slightest shred of evidence. Looked at from a different perspective, however, the paradoxes associated with religious belief are not so much symptoms of irrationality but conditions of understanding, as they caution us against false analogies between the reality of God and that which exists within the horizon of our sense experience. As Weil's *Notebook* entries make clear, her own thoughts on the matter are inspired by the biblical depiction of God as a *Deus absconditus*, who must necessarily be absent from the world we inhabit. 'Verily thou art a God that hides thyself', writes the prophet Isaiah,[16] and Weil agrees that the remark expresses a fundamental truth about the believer's relation to God. It is a truth with which R. S. Thomas also grapples in 'The Absence':

It is this great absence
that is like a presence, that compels
me to address it without hope
of a reply. It is a room I enter

from which someone has just
gone, the vestibule for the arrival
of one who has not yet come.
I modernise the anachronism

of my language, but he is no more here
than before. Genes and molecules
have no more power to call
him up than the incense of the Hebrews

at their altars. My equations fail
as my words do. What resources have I
other than the emptiness without him of my whole
being, a vacuum he may not abhor?[17]

Even the poet is lost for words when meditating on the paradox
that God's 'great absence' is nevertheless 'like a presence'. Within
the realm of human relations, the absence of a beloved individual
leaves us with a powerful sense of emptiness and deprivation, a void
that could only be filled by the presence of the beloved. When the
object of our love is God, however, our attitude should be exactly
the opposite: in so far as absence *is* the mode of his being, that
absence should engender neither lament nor despair.

If we find it difficult to adopt this attitude, it is probably because
we are still in the grip of the false impression that God's absence is a
form of wilful and uncaring abandonment, coldly indifferent to
supplications seemingly made 'without hope of a reply'. But, as
Weil reminds us in her *Notebooks*, 'the apparent absence of God in
this world is the actual reality of God. The same is true for everything. Whatever is an appearance is unreality.'[18] Her insistence that
God's reality and the world's unreality entail each other is, of
course, not merely a point of conceptual clarification, but a serious
exhortation to abandon all counterfeit values for the genuine love
of God. In so far as this endeavour involves a radical change in a
person's perspective on life, we can also say, with her, that 'to think
on God, to love God, is nothing else than a certain way of thinking
on the world'.[19] But now we need to ask: can such a change in
perspective be pursued at will? How does one come to embrace it?

This returns us to Weil's misgivings about the idea that one can
'search for God', and to her contention that coming to believe in
God is not a matter of being persuaded by evidence, justification, or
proof. Once again, one is struck by the spiritual kinship between

Weil and Wittgenstein on this issue, and by the way in which these observations by Wittgenstein could well serve as a summary of Weil's own conclusions:

> A proof of God ought really to be something by means of which you can convince yourself of God's existence. But I think that believers who offered such proofs wanted to analyse & make a case for their 'belief' with their intellect, although they themselves would never have arrived at belief by way of such proofs. 'Convincing someone of God's existence' is something you might do by means of a certain upbringing, shaping his life in such & such a way. Life can educate you to 'believing in God'. And experiences too are what do this but not visions, or other sense experiences, which show us the 'existence of this being', but e.g. sufferings of various sorts. And they do not show us God as a sense experience does an object ... Experiences, thoughts, – life can force this concept on us.[20]

In the light of these remarks, we can understand why the suggestion that one can embark on a search for God strikes Weil as no less absurd than a conscious quest for the kind of moral awakening that would convert a militant racist into a staunch egalitarian, or that would turn a connoisseur and lover of fine meats into a resolute vegetarian and fervent defender of animal rights. Such moral and spiritual awakenings are not subject to the will, but, as Weil never tires of pointing out, matters of grace:

> With all things, it is always what comes to us from outside, freely and by surprise as a gift from heaven without our having sought it, that brings us pure joy. In the same way real good can only come from outside ourselves, never from our own effort.[21]

The joyful acceptance of the greatest goods in life as 'gifts from heaven' is of deep spiritual significance, not only because it expresses the realisation that there are limits to our intellectual, moral, and spiritual endeavours, but because it instils in us a profound sense of humility and awe towards the God on whom we depend for our very being and flourishing. This is why the notion of grace is not merely a peripheral concept in religious belief, but central to an understanding of its very nature. The attitude of one who thought that the good in his life, from the moral steadfastness that informs his decisions and actions, to his professional accomplishments, material possessions, good health, and social reputation, were entirely the result of his own efforts and careful planning, would be very different from the attitude of a religious believer who ascribed everything to God – including the strength to make an effort in the first place and the outcome of his endeavours, all of which might have been thwarted by forces beyond his control. To say that God's grace is needed for human flourishing is, of course, not to endorse the kind of fatalism that results in idleness or passivity. When Weil says that 'to search is to impede rather than to facilitate God's operation',[22] she is merely drawing attention to the peculiar difficulties involved in coming to see the world as God's creation, and to the limitations of the intellect in this connection:

> It has nothing to do with an intellectual process in the present-day sense. The intelligence has nothing to discover, it has only to clear the ground. It is only good for servile tasks.[23]

On its own, the intellect can no more lead us to belief in God – by way of elaborate arguments or sophisticated attempts at rational justification, for example – than could a *specifiable* set of experiences, even though believers may feel obligated to justify their beliefs once they have come to see things from a religious point of view, forgetting the fact, rightly noted by Wittgenstein, that 'Experiences, thoughts, – life can force this concept [God] on us'. What we need to guard against, then, is the idea that coming to see the world as God's creation must be *either* an affair of the heart *or* an intellectual matter, and that our primary task consists in specifying the relevant experiences and/or arguments that will take us there. We only need to recall Socrates' quixotic battles against the confusions of his interlocutors, or our earlier discussion of the contrast between Castorp's enlightenment and Eichmann's ignorance, to realise that genuine spiritual conversions require not merely *experiences* of various kinds, but a response whose character depends very much on the spiritual condition of the person who has those experiences. If the response turns out to be a religious one, then this will itself be viewed as 'a gift from heaven', as the product of a fortuitous encounter between a particular individual and the circumstances in which he finds himself. The role of the intellect in all this is 'to clear the ground', as it were, by ensuring that we do not fall into conceptual confusion, self-deception, or daydreaming, especially in relation to matters of the spirit.

As for the so-called 'problem of faith', construed in terms of practical doubts about God's reality, Weil thinks it 'does not arise':

> For any man of whom God has taken possession, the doubt concerning the reality of God is purely abstract and verbal, much more abstract and verbal than the doubt concerning the reality of the things of sense.[24]

Thus, the intelligence can no more undermine genuine belief in God than it can compel us to embrace such belief in the first place, and Weil consequently takes the claim that we may cease to believe in God on purely intellectual grounds to be just as unconvincing as the attempt to justify that belief by rational argument. But are there not believers who claim to have lost their faith on such grounds – because they came to see, for example, that the existence of evil in the world was irreconcilable with belief in a benevolent God? In elaboration of the above quotation, Weil would say that we must be careful to distinguish between the loss of faith, on the one hand, and what someone would say – both to himself and to others – about that loss, on the other. It is true that, when someone realises that he can no longer think of his life as a gift from God, say, or ceases to value something he had always treasured, or has fallen out of love with someone whom he thought he could not live without, he may well feel under an obligation to explain the change of attitude in terms of 'reasons' – e.g. 'I no longer love her, because . . .' But why should we think of these reasons as causes, rather than as rationalisations, of his loss, prompted by the natural craving for explanations and the equally natural reluctance to face the disturbing experience of the inexplicable?

Losing faith in God, i.e. ceasing to attach meaning to the pictures, rituals, and forms of expression that previously informed one's thoughts and actions, seems much more akin to falling out of love with someone than to relinquishing a deeply cherished investment project because there are new and compelling (financial) reasons for abandoning it. What makes the former experiences *tragic* is not so much that they befall us unexpectedly, though this may also be true, but that they may occur in the absence of a rational explanation – hence Simone Weil's insistence that reason and rationality can neither compel us to love God, nor force us to entertain doubts about his reality, once he has taken possession of us.

The Christian attitude

Simone Weil did not consciously search for God, then, and left the theoretical debate over his existence alone, convinced that it was more important to adopt 'the best attitude with regard to the problems of this world', and that 'such an attitude does not depend upon the solution of the problem of God'.[25] Weil has no doubts about what that attitude should be: 'I always adopted the Christian attitude as the only possible one. I might say that I was born, I grew up, and I always remained within the Christian inspiration.'[26] The name of God did not come to hold a prominent place in her thoughts until 1941, but her conduct was nevertheless informed by ideas that were deeply rooted in the Christian tradition.[27] Some of these had always been part of her outlook, while others imposed themselves on her through experiences of various kinds, including the three contacts with Catholicism that, in her own estimation, proved to be particularly significant. These contacts, which occurred during her visits to Portugal (1934/35), Assisi (1937), and Solesmes (1938),[28] not only deepened her understanding of the relation between human affliction and God's love, but generated a habit of regular, attentive prayer, and firmly anchored her faith in an unexpected mystical experience of Christ's presence.

Quite independently of what these encounters with Catholicism taught her, the Christian attitude which she insists had always permeated her life revealed itself in, among other things, 'the spirit of poverty' epitomised in St Francis of Assisi, whose life, she hoped, would be forced on her as well; in the Christian idea of love for one's neighbour, associated with the idea of justice; in 'the duty of acceptance in all that concerns the will of God', or what the Stoic philosopher Marcus Aurelius described as *amor fati*; and in the idea of purity, which took hold of her at the age of sixteen as she was contemplating a mountain landscape.[29] 'That', so Weil observes, 'is why it never occurred to me that I could enter the Christian community. I had the idea that I was born inside.'[30]

The 'Christian inspiration', God, and the Incarnation

But can there plausibly be a *Christian* attitude towards life that makes no reference to *God*? Indeed, if one's thoughts and actions are oriented towards Christ, doesn't one also have to think of him as the *Son* of God? Can one be a Christian without believing in the Incarnation? Weil's answer to the last question, in particular, is complex and will be discussed in more detail below. What is already clear, however, is that, if a life can be lived in the Christian spirit *without* involving the thought of Christ as a supernatural incarnation of God, then presumably even a certain kind of atheist could live in this spirit. And this is what Weil seems to be suggesting, though it must be remembered that she is speaking from the point of view of someone whose own worldview has come to revolve around Christ and the rich conceptual tapestry surrounding the Christian, in particular the Catholic, faith. An atheist, by comparison, who does *not* typically think of his existence in any of the terms or imagery characteristic of traditional Christianity – e.g. God's incarnation, the Passion, Judgement Day, redemption, salvation, resurrection, etc. – would be reluctant to describe *himself* as a Christian, though he might well recognise certain *analogies* between his own attitude to life and that of a Christian believer.

Weil does not deny any of this, of course, nor does she want to insist, even more absurdly, that all atheists are really Christians in disguise. Her point is rather that the general intellectual, ethical, and spiritual orientation of a life – one that is marked by such attributes as truthfulness, self-renunciation, humility, gratitude for life, self-sacrificial love of neighbour, poverty, etc. – may bear such a striking resemblance to that of a Christian believer that it would be natural to speak of it as an example of *implicit faith*, of the way in which the Holy Spirit may inform the lives even of those who never consciously think of Christ, the Incarnation, or God. Of course, the converse is also true: not everyone who has been received into the Church through baptism, and who continues to share in its celebratory and sacrificial rituals, is necessarily a follower of Christ, regardless of how fervently he may protest that he is. A genuinely Christian life manifests, among many other things, unfailing obedience to the requirements of love and, as Weil insists, only 'those who fulfill Christ's commands love him – even if they do not believe in the Incarnation'.[31]

In addition to the considerations already mentioned, Weil's talk of implicit faith is motivated by a deeper concern which, incidentally, also led the German theologian Karl Rahner to propagate the idea of the 'anonymous Christian'. Reflecting on the spiritual predicament of those who find themselves outside the (Christian) Church, Rahner asks:

> Can the Christian believe even for a moment that the overwhelming mass of his brothers, not only those before the

appearance of Christ right back to the most distant past (whose horizons are constantly extended by palaeontology) but also those of the present and of the future before us, are unquestionably and in principle excluded from the fulfilment of their lives and condemned to eternal meaninglessness? He must reject any suggestion, and his faith is itself in agreement with his doing so. For the scriptures tell him expressly that God wants everyone to be saved (1 Tm 2:4).[32]

Given that, in the Christian tradition, salvation is only possible by reference to Christ, it seems to follow that those who were born outside the Christian tradition must either be doomed, or else granted salvation in a way that honours the universality of Christ's salvific action. It is in this context that Rahner introduces the concept of the anonymous Christian:

We prefer the terminology according to which that man is called an 'anonymous Christian' who on the one hand has de facto accepted of his freedom this gracious self-offering on God's part through faith, hope, and love, while on the other he is absolutely not yet a Christian at the social level (through baptism and membership of the Church) or in the sense of having consciously objectified his Christianity to himself in his own mind (by explicit Christian faith resulting from having hearkened to the explicit Christian message). We might therefore put it as follows: the 'anonymous Christian' in our sense of the term is the pagan after the beginning of the Christian mission, who lives in the state of Christ's grace through faith, hope and love, yet who has no explicit knowledge of the fact that his life is orientated in grace-given salvation to Jesus Christ.[33]

The point of Weil's and Rahner's remarks on implicit faith and anonymous Christians is not to deliver a procedure for spiritual self-assessment, but to ensure that Christ's redeeming action can be seen to extend well beyond the boundaries of the Christian church, to all those who, while not Christians, still live 'in the state of Christ's grace'.

Now, Weil's earlier claim that a true love of Christ need not involve belief in the Incarnation will strike many readers as both unorthodox and indefensible, not least because the recognition of Jesus *as* Christ seems to be so intimately connected with the idea that he *is* God's incarnation. Indeed, would Jesus' words and

90

commands carry the authority they do if they were not thought to emanate from the Son of God?

If Weil rejects these objections as hasty, it is not only because she plausibly holds that pure manifestations of self-renunciation and neighbourly love must already have existed long before the birth of Jesus, and that it would be presumptuous of contemporary Christians to accord their pre-Christian neighbours no more than an imperfect or deficient understanding of God's will merely because they had not been witnesses to its incarnation in Christ. Weil also wants us to note that spiritual proximity to Christ is not so much a function of the extent to which one consciously affirms this or that article of Church dogma, or engages in regular incantations of particular words or phrases addressed to God, but a matter of living in the *spirit* of Christ's commands. Consonant with all this, she frankly admits that, prior to her mystical experiences at Solesmes in 1938, 'the very name of God had no part in my thoughts',[34] and that, up until September 1941, 'I had never once prayed in all my life, at least not in the literal sense of the word. I had never said any words to God, either out loud or mentally. I had never pronounced a liturgical prayer.'[35] On the question of the Incarnation, she likewise confesses, 'I never wondered whether Jesus was or was not an incarnation of God; but in fact I was incapable of thinking of him without thinking of him as God.'[36]

Apart from shedding further light on Weil's spiritual development, the preceding remarks also invite reflection on what is involved in the formation of religious concepts – e.g. to what extent they precede religious practice, or are the product of far more primitive, unreflective responses to particular individuals, places, or events – and on the *spiritual* significance of the elaborate dogmatism propagated by institutionalised Christianity:

> St. John says: 'Whosoever believes Jesus to be the Christ is born of God.' Thus whoever believes that, even if he assents to nothing else of what is affirmed by the Church, possesses the true faith. ... Furthermore the Church, by adding to the Trinity, the Incarnation and the Redemption, other articles of faith, has gone against the New Testament.[37]

For Weil, to see Jesus as the Christ is, first and foremost, to invest his life and teaching with a certain kind of *transcendence*, and when the Church seeks to circumscribe that transcendence in terms of a triadic relation (God, Jesus, Holy Spirit), or by invoking the notion of incarnation, then this is both appropriate and spiritually edifying. If, on the other hand, a Church council defines 'faith' as unquestioning adherence to all of its doctrines, then this seems to Weil to be 'very far removed from that of St. John, for whom faith was purely and simply belief in the Incarnation of the Son of God in the person of Jesus'.[38]

Whether the Church has, in fact, distorted the Gospel of St John in the way Weil suggests will be taken up later, in connection with her more general criticisms of institutionalised religion. First, it is necessary to elaborate on the notion of transcendence, partly because its meaning is still obscure, and partly because there is a way of taking Weil's remarks about life in the spirit of Christ that would, in fact, be diametrically opposed to her views. If she is interpreted as saying that 'the spirit of Christ' is simply synonymous with 'a high standard of moral excellence', 'uncommonly virtuous behaviour', or the like, then it looks as if humanity's spiritual history could, in principle, be understood quite independently of Christ. But this is precisely what Weil does *not* want to say, as it would turn Christ into a mere metaphor of moral or other kinds of value, and thus into an aspect of the worldly or 'immanent'. For Weil, Christ's transcendence involves the idea that he is *eternal*, and it is precisely because his redeeming action is of universal salvific significance that he can save all those who live in his spirit.[39] In other words, the figure of Christ is the key to the meaning of life, precisely because he is not reducible to anything *in* the world; only that which properly transcends the world can infuse it with ultimate and objective significance.

The Jewish thinker Martin Buber helps us appreciate this point with a literary example. Rightly noting that 'complete inclusion of the divine in the sphere of the human self abolishes its divinity',[40] he contrasts the religious language of the classical dramatist Aeschylus with that of Euripides, the last of the great Athenian poets. In Aeschylus' play *Agamemnon*, for example, the chorus proclaims:

Zeus, whoever he is,
If it pleases him so to be called,
With this name I invoke him.[41]

The crucial phrase here is 'whoever he is'. How is it to be interpreted? Buber teases out its meaning with another fragment from Aeschylus' work, according to which 'Zeus is all and what is more than all' – an addendum which, on Buber's view, not only yields a deep and substantial sense of transcendence, but a harmonious relation with the immanent:

> Here, immanence is united with transcendence. But in connection with the following passage, 'If it pleases him so to be called', the scholiast rightly refers to the sentence in Plato's *Cratylus*: 'We know neither the nature nor the true names of the gods'. The next sentence explains that just for this reason we address them in prayer by the names they like.[42]

The passage from Aeschylus may now be contrasted with a scene from Euripides' *Trojan Women*, where Hecuba calls on Zeus with the following words:

> O Foundation of the earth and above it throned,
> Whoever thou art, beyond our mind's poor grasp,
> Whether Zeus or Fate or spirit of men,
> I implore thee.[43]

As Buber points out, the similar beginnings of the two quotations should not blind us to the fact that, in the latter, 'the religious situation is abolished by the total immanence which is considered in what follows as one of the possibilities. As if one could pray to "the spirit of men"!'[44] The spirit of man, even humanity as such, cannot be the measure of transcendence, in spite of what Euripides' language suggests:

> We are the slaves of gods, whatever gods may be.
> Zeus, whosoever Zeus indeed may be, –
> Only through hearsay know I aught of him.[45]

Buber finds in Euripides' language of the transcendent the gradual erosion of an earlier, spiritually much richer, conception of the divine, which saw the gods as irreducibly other, and man as appropriately subordinated to a will that was 'higher' than his own. In Buber's words:

> It is a decisively significant way which leads from 'whoever he is' of Aeschylus to the seemingly similar 'whoever Zeus indeed may be' of the last of the great tragedians. ... It is the situation of the man who no longer experiences the divine as standing over against him. ... Although the chorus of Aeschylus also speaks of

God in the third person, it makes a genuine invocation from human to divine being. On the other hand, in the pathos of Hecuba, despite its threefold saying of 'Thou', no true Thou is in reality implied. [45]

Far from invoking a genuine 'Thou', Hecuba's language ends up pointing at humanity itself, and thus at something which, by its very nature, necessarily falls short of all that we associate with the divine. Reflecting on this a little further, we can also see more clearly now what Weil means by 'spiritual' in her *Spiritual Autobiography* and elsewhere in her writings. In ordinary, everyday discourse, the word is frequently used to mean simply the opposite of 'material' or 'physical', namely, that dimension of our being which concerns such 'immaterial' phenomena as concepts, mental imagery, reason, or an individual's particular psychological makeup.

But, as C. S. Lewis has rightly emphasised, 'what is "spiritual" in this sense is not necessarily good'.[47] When the word 'spiritual' appears in the reflections of Christian writers, by contrast, its sense is internally connected with goodness, on the one hand, and with grateful acceptance of the gifts of divine grace, on the other.[48] Weil's spiritual autobiography duly reflects the interdependence of these ideas, through linking their meaning to the notion of a transcendent God who, as the very embodiment of the Good, allows us to experience its earthly manifestations as gifts of grace. On this account, the ideas of goodness and grace *necessarily* point towards a transcendent reality, and the epiphanic experience of Jesus *as* Christ constitutes its paradigmatic recognition. The concepts of transcendence and absolute goodness, then, are intimately connected, and would be regarded by Weil as important features of any perspective on the world that could properly be called religious.

Having gone some way towards elucidating the *kind* of transcendence involved in religious belief, we must now turn to the other side of this spiritual coin, and elaborate some more on Weil's understanding of the Incarnation. The difficulty here is that, since she does not present us with a detailed and systematic treatment of the subject, our only interpretative signposts are the scattered remarks in the *First and Last Notebooks* (1933–39/1942–43), the *Notebooks* (1940–42), and her *Letter to a Priest* (1942).[49] Moreover, even if we are able to piece together some of Weil's reflections on this complex issue, we should not expect her observations to yield a tidy 'theory' or even a coherent 'account' of the Incarnation. Weil finds it extremely difficult to express herself clearly about 'these almost inexpressible things',[50] and our own predicament is no different. Her reflections should therefore be taken, not as pieces of a spiritual mosaic which she had no time to complete, but as fragments of a meditation that is necessarily open-ended. The following observations indicate the general direction of Weil's thought.

Inspired by Plato's conception of beautiful objects as transient manifestations of an unchanging and transcendent archetype,[51] Weil thinks that beauty is the only aspect of God's nature to be reflected in the material universe, whereas other aspects of his being, including goodness and justice, 'can only be incarnated in a human being'.[52] Indeed, the experience of a human face, a painting, a landscape, or a piece of music as beautiful strikes her as an 'experimental proof of the possibility of incarnation';[53] it takes us beyond the domain of the earthly and temporal, into that of the transcendent and immutable, somewhat analogously to the way in which certain moral requirements – the Decalogue, for example – come to be seen as timelessly and unconditionally binding.

Either case could be regarded as a kind of incarnation: beauty becomes incarnate in material objects, and goodness in certain kinds of human action, and neither of these attributes are mere projections of the human mind. On the contrary, Weil is adamant that any genuine work of art, for example, 'is an attempt to transport into a limited quantity of matter, modelled by man, an image of the infinite beauty of the entire universe',[54] so there is a sense in which the beauty of the universe itself does *not* depend on our perception of it. The universe is beautiful because it is God's creation, not because we happen to find this or that aspect of it aesthetically pleasing. And indeed, if beauty *is* a true attribute of the *objective* ground of all being – i.e. God – it could hardly be reduced to a *subjective* feature of human experience, and we shall see later how this insight also has important implications for how we are to regard the existence of evil in the world.

In addition, we need to recall here that, for Weil, beauty always goes hand in hand with a certain kind of *order*. To use one of her own examples: on one level of description, there is no difference between the actions of a child who draws in the sand, and the movements of Michelangelo's hand as he is working on a painting, or between the chattering of children and the recitation of a poem.[55] However, what is missing from the chatter is precisely what we think essential to the poem, viz. a certain form, structure, or *order*. As Weil puts it: '[V]erse has fixed laws, and the most beautiful verses are the most rigid from the point of view of form. ... It is paradoxical that a poet expresses himself better in following laws than in not following them.'[56] Similarly with Michelangelo's paintings and sculptures: they represent authentic art because their creation is guided by the same sense of equilibrium, harmony, and proportion that constitutes an essential aspect of the beauty of the world, and what makes Michelangelo an artistic genius is precisely this ability to transform every *particular* painting or sculpture into a mirror of that *universal* beauty.[57] What is required for such transformations, however, is always 'a transcendent inspiration', a gift for discerning the 'transcendent model' whose physical incarnation is the world itself,[58] and hence a certain kind of *religious* sensibility.

This requirement will strike many, especially the friends of avant-garde art, as narrow and conservative, but it should be found congenial by anyone who agrees with Weil that aesthetic, ethical, and religious sensibilities are not only interdependent, but manifestations of the kind of harmony and equilibrium that already inspired the greatest artists of ancient Greece. Weil's judgement on most of the artworks produced in her own time, though, is rather sobering. In her pre-war *Notebook* (1933–39), she observes that it is precisely because 'modern life is given over to excess' and because 'there is no more equilibrium anywhere' that art has become so decadent.[59] For a deeper appreciation of this verdict, one would, of course, have to look at some concrete examples and compare the aesthetic ideals of Renaissance artists like Michelangelo and Dürer, for instance, with those of Surrealists such as Max Ernst and René Magritte; or contrast the principles of melody, harmony, and rhythm discernible in the compositions of Monteverdi, Bach, or Mozart,[60] with those betrayed – in both senses of the word – by contemporary pop music.

We cannot dwell on this issue here, but should note two points for further reflection. The first is raised in Weil's essay 'The Responsibility of Writers' (1941), and has a direct bearing on her evaluation of the Surrealist movement as such. In this connection, Weil writes:

Dadaism and surrealism ... represented the intoxication of total license, the intoxication in which the mind wallows when it has made a clean sweep of value and surrendered to the immediate. ... The surrealists have set up non-oriented thought as a model; they have chosen the total absence of value as their supreme value. Men have always been intoxicated by license, which is why, throughout history, towns have been sacked. But there has not always been a literary equivalent for the sacking of towns. Surrealism is such an equivalent.[61]

The Surrealist movement, which developed out of Dadaism ('dada' is French for 'hobby horse'), flourished mainly between 1920 and 1940, and counted the poet André Breton, who also published *The Surrealist Manifesto* in 1924, among its leading literary representatives. Deliberately rejecting aesthetic orthodoxy and 'bourgeois' values, the Surrealists sought to blur the distinction between the conscious and the unconscious and, under the influence of Freud's writings, to inject an element of the irrational into what they perceived as an overly 'rationalistic' conception of existence. However, in Weil's view the Surrealists' radical rejection of aesthetic and moral tradition also resulted in nihilistic licentiousness and 'non-oriented thought', and thus in artworks which meant what they said, viz. nothing.

The second point, provocatively articulated by Roger Scruton, concerns the aesthetic value of certain types of music, including contemporary pop music:

Even when pop aims to be lyrical, melody is synthesized from standardized phrases, which could be rearranged in any order without losing or gaining effect. It is not that such music is tuneless: rather that the tune comes from elsewhere, like food from the supermarket shelf, to be heated in the microwave.[62]

But melodic impoverishment is not the only thing that worries Scruton about pop music. Equally disquieting, in his view, is the use of instruments that displace the human voice and mechanize our experiences of sound to the point of alienating us even from our own natures:

The electric guitar ... is also a machine, which distorts and amplifies the sound, lifting it out of the realm of human noises. If a machine could sing, it would sound like an electric guitar. Techno music *is* the voice of the machine, triumphing over the human utterance and cancelling its preeminent claim to our attention. In such music we encounter the background noise of modern life, but suddenly projected into the foreground, so as to fill all the auditory space. However much you listen to this music, you will never hear it as you hear the human voice; not even when it sounds so loudly that you can hear nothing else. You are overhearing the machine, as it discourses in the moral void.[63]

Whatever one may think of Scruton's comments on the electric guitar, his general point about the harmonic triteness of pop music and the subjugation of the human voice and body to the mechanised sound of the techno beat certainly merits further reflection. Could a Christian who believes that she has been created in God's image, and that her vocation consists in being true to that image, allow her humanity to be suppressed by the movements of a machine? Do certain kinds of music alienate us from ourselves? When Weil writes that 'all art of the first order testifies to the fact of the Incarnation',[64] she is prompting us to measure our own aesthetic orientation against the standards set by precisely such art.

Unlike those who think that beauty lies entirely in the eye of the beholder, and is therefore just a matter of subjective preference, Weil believes, not only that aesthetic judgements can be just as *objective* as moral judgements, but that the character of our aesthetic experience also says something important about our relation to God:

> If the beautiful is the real presence of God in matter and if contact with the beautiful is a sacrament in the full sense of the word, how is it that there are so many perverted aesthetes? Nero. Is it like the hunger of those who frequent black masses for the consecrated hosts? Or is it, more probably, because these people do not devote themselves to what is genuinely beautiful, but to a bad imitation? For, just as there is an art which is divine, so there is one which is demoniacal. It was no doubt the latter that Nero loved. A great deal of our art is of the devil. A person who is passionately fond of music may quite well be a perverted person – but I should find it hard to believe this of any one who thirsted for Gregorian chanting.[65]

Our discussion started out with Weil's view of beauty as a kind of incarnation, and we can see now why she thinks this starting point so fruitful. Through it, we have been led to the distinction between divine art and demonic imitations of it; to the idea that an encounter with beauty has *sacramental* character; to the insight that, just as God combines within himself the attributes of beauty and goodness, so proper aesthetic appreciation in human beings is bound to go hand in hand with a certain spiritual and ethical orientation; and finally to the practical exhortation that we must be vigilant not to be seduced by art that, contrary to all appearances, is of the devil. What is particularly valuable in Weil's treatment of these complex matters is her acknowledgement that, in assessing our spiritual proximity to Christ, ethical considerations need not be the sole criterion of sober judgement, and that, if we want to convey a true picture of reality, we must resort to aesthetic categories as well. For when we see the material universe under the aspect of beauty, we also find that some of the (sceptical) questions we would otherwise have been tempted to raise – e.g. about the occurrence of natural disasters, etc. – can be silenced. But we shall return to this issue later.

6

Religious Reflection (2): Christ, Krishna, and the Old Testament

On the subject of the Incarnation, we can now reiterate our earlier concern: if the universe is an incarnation – or better: reflection – of one of God's attributes, then, unless we allow for multiple universes existing in different regions of space-time, it is clear that this incarnation must be a *unique* and singular event. Does Simone Weil believe that the *ethical* analogue of this *aesthetic* incarnation is similarly unique? In other words: does she think that God's pure and perfect justice can only be incarnated in *one* human being? The answer, as C. S. Lewis correctly observes, is also of crucial importance for our understanding of God's relation to his creation: 'If the thing happened, it was the central event in the history of the Earth – the very thing that the whole story has been about.'[1]

Indeed, when the Catholic Catechism speaks of 'the unique and altogether singular event of the Incarnation of the Son of God',[2] and refers to Jesus Christ as 'the one and only mediator between God and man',[3] it is evident that the uniqueness of the Incarnation, the recognition of Jesus as Christ, and our understanding of God's revelation in human history are all closely connected. To hypothesise about multiple incarnations would be to imagine that God had several Sons, which would in turn create serious difficulties for the doctrine of the Trinity, according to which God, his Son, and the Holy Spirit are *three* divine persons, not five or nineteen. On this point, Christian doctrine would unequivocally reject the kind of view articulated by Immanuel Kant, who argued that

> the doctrine of the Trinity, taken literally, has *no practical relevance at all*, even if we think we understand it ... Whether we are to worship three or ten persons in the Deity makes no difference: the pupil will implicitly accept one as readily as the other because he has no concept at all of a number of persons in one God (hypostases), and still more so because this distinction can make no difference in his rules of conduct.[4]

Given Kant's pervasive influence on the development of Weil's thought, it is tempting to think that she would agree with him on this matter. However, her remarks on the Trinity – most notably in the *Notebooks* and *Intimations of Christianity* – not only suggest otherwise, but reveal a much subtler understanding of the Trinity than Kant displays in the above quotation. While it is true that the mystery of the Trinity is difficult to conceptualise, and that a life in Christ is a *practical* rather than an intellectual affair, Weil strongly disagrees that belief in the Trinity 'has no practical relevance at all', let alone that it could be dispensed with altogether.

On the contrary, apart from prompting the believer to meditate on the Incarnation 'and *consequently* the Creation',[5] the Trinity is, in fact, '*indispensable* to the Greek and Christian notion of Justice':[6] on reflection, we find that the notion of justice is intimately bound up with that of *equality*, and that there could be no purer manifestation of the latter than the perfect equality and 'supreme harmony'[7] which characterises the relation between the three persons of the Trinity.[8] Clearly – and *pace* Kant – the recognition of these conceptual connections is also bound to have a *practical* impact on the lives of those who believe in the triune God.

In this connection, Weil is struck once more by the spiritual depth of Plato, who not only 'recognised the essential truth, namely, that God is the Good', but who, 'by allusions in his works, pointed to the dogmas of the Trinity, Mediation, the Incarnation, the Passion, and to the notions of grace and salvation through love.'[9] Weil detects one such allusion towards the end of Book V of Plato's *Republic*,[10] where Socrates raises an important question about the relation between the ideal of justice and its earthly manifestations. 'If we find what justice is, should we hold that the just man must in no way differ from that, but must be in all regards absolutely just?', Socrates asks his interlocutor Glaucon, and it is clear that this question about 'what the ideal of a perfectly just man is, in case he might exist, and what he would be if he did exist'[11] is identical with the question of what a true incarnation of God would be like. Weil herself interprets the passage as follows:

> Even the most just men are but close to justice, they are not in every respect that which justice is. But one must also conceive what the perfectly just man would be like, should he happen to be born, without going into the question of whether such a thing is possible or not. Now, this man would be in every respect the same thing as justice ..., in every respect like unto justice; therefore, in spite of the fact that he was on earth, he would belong to those realities which lie on the other side of the sky.[12]

Of course, it is one thing to agree that *if* there was an incarnation of divine justice here below, it would have to be, not merely an approximation to absolute goodness, but a perfect manifestation of it; and another to insist that there has, in fact, been such an incarnation. Here, Weil sides with Plato in thinking that 'the model for justice is *a just man*',[13] not merely an abstract idea:

> The ideal model for relatively just men can only be a perfectly just man. Relatively just men exist. If their model is to be real, he must have an earthly existence at a certain point in space, and at a certain moment of time. There is no other reality for a man. If the ideal cannot have this existence, it is nothing but an abstraction.[14]

Thus, the Incarnation is not merely a logical possibility, or a metaphor for an abstract ideal of human conduct, but a reality in which 'the divine model, the perfectly just man, is the mediator between just men and God'.[15] Moreover – and this is another Platonic intimation of Christian doctrine – Weil argues that a truly authentic incarnation of perfect justice can only take the form it took with Christ, viz. naked and stripped of all appearance of earthly prestige:

> In order that divine justice may be a model for men to imitate, it is not enough that it should be incarnate in a man. In that man, moreover, the authenticity of perfect justice must be manifest.

For that, the justice in him must be seen without prestige, naked without honour, divested of all the brilliance which the reputation of justice gives.[16]

What makes Christ's justice truly *authentic* is, paradoxically enough, that it was veiled behind the appearance of injustice – the most righteous man on Earth, treated like a common criminal and abandoned even by his friends. The paradoxical nature of Christ's predicament reflects a more general problem: since injustice may appear in the guise of justice, and true justice may be concealed behind the appearance of injustice, it is difficult to tell the two apart. However, if true justice presents itself 'naked' and without any disguise, as it did in Christ's Passion, then anyone who possesses the light of grace will be able to recognise it:

During the days when Christ was, as Plato would have him, completely stripped of all appearance of justice, even his friends themselves were no longer wholly conscious of his being perfectly righteous. Otherwise could they have slept while he suffered, could they have fled, have denied him? After the Resurrection the infamous character of his ordeal was effaced by glory, and today, across twenty centuries of adoration, the degradation which is the very essence of the Passion is hardly felt by us. We think now only of the suffering, and of that but vaguely, for the sufferings which we imagine are always lacking in gravity. We no longer imagine the dying Christ as a common criminal.[17]

When Weil says that our representation of Christ's suffering lacks gravity, she is not merely thinking of the physical aspect of Jesus' ordeal, such as the protracted torture he underwent before he was nailed to the cross. Any lack of imagination in this regard could easily be remedied with the kind of graphic, cinematographic depiction of ancient Roman torture techniques to be found in Mel Gibson's film *The Passion of the Christ*, for example, but this would not (yet) capture the full extent of the *degradation* Jesus suffered. For that goes well beyond the experience of horrendous physical pain and involves, not only the thought of suffering a grave injustice – a source of torment in itself – but the humiliation of being lowered in the eyes of his fellow-men to something barely recognisable as human.

Even so, Christ's love for his Father was not crushed, and if the Passion is of such central importance to the Christian faith, it is not least because of what it reveals about the nature of that love. Weil acknowledges that this kind of love *is* singular and unique, but – and this is where her views begin to diverge from standard Christian doctrine – she would find it hard to believe that, *therefore*, the Catholic Catechism must be right in describing Christ's incarnation as an 'altogether singular event', unrepeated and unrepeatable at any other time in human history.[18]

Thus, she wonders whether Noah in the Old Testament may not also have been an incarnation,[19] and whether the New Testament remarks on Melchizedek, the mysterious priest-king of Salem who brings bread and wine to Abraham as the latter returns from Damascus, do not suggest another instance of the Word becoming flesh.[20] In the Epistle to the Hebrews, we read:

> Let us note that the name *Melchizedek* means King of Justice, and that *king of Salem* means King of Peace. There is no mention of father, mother or genealogy; nothing is said about the beginning or the end of his life. In this he is the figure of the Son of God, the priest who remains for ever.[21]

For Weil, such words 'seem clearly to establish the fact that it is a question of an incarnation',[22] rather than an example of an uncommonly righteous individual.

But it is not only certain characters in the Old Testament who strike her as divine incarnations. In her *Letter to a Priest*, written in the autumn of 1942, just before she left New York for London, she contends that 'we do not know for certain that there have not been incarnations previous to that of Jesus, and that Osiris in Egypt, Krishna in India were not of that number'.[23] What intrigued Weil about the Osiris cult, which flourished in Egypt over 2,000 years before the incarnation of Christ, was not only the idea of divine sonship – the Egyptians believed that, at death, their earthly king became Osiris, the god of the underworld, and that, on ascending to the throne, the dead king's son became Horus, the god of the sky, and son of Osiris – but its striking proximity to the spirit of Christian worship:

> The Egyptian Book of the Dead, at least three thousand years old, and doubtless very much older, is filled with evangelic charity. (The dead man says to Osiris: 'Lord of Truth, I bring thee the truth ... I have destroyed evil for thee ... I have killed no man. I have made no man weep. I have let no man suffer

hunger. I have never been the cause of a master's doing harm to his slave. I have never made any man afraid. I have never adopted a haughty tone. I have never turned a deaf ear to just and true words. I have never put my name forward for honours. I have not spurned God in His manifestations. . . .')[24]

Weil is not sure whether *all* Egyptian gods were divine incarnations, or whether Osiris, who was worshipped throughout Egypt, was the only one, but it does seem to her 'irrefutable' that Osiris, Melchizedek, and Christ *are* such incarnations.[25] Commenting on Weil's remarks about ancient Egypt, Father Perrin has objected that her grasp of these matters was 'very deficient in many points', and that she was 'content to base her admiration of the whole of the Egyptian religion solely on the *Book of the Dead*'.[26]

Now, it is true that Weil's knowledge of the subject was largely derived from the *Book of the Dead* and from Plutarch's studies of Egyptian religion, most notably *Isis and Osiris*, but the central question is not *how much* she read, but *how well* she had read the texts she explicitly mentions, and whether there are independent confirmations of her interpretation of these texts. In this connection, the work of the German Catholic theologian Eugen Drewermann (1940–) could serve as a forceful contemporary endorsement of Weil's thought, both in terms of the examples he uses in illustration of ancient Egyptian religiosity, and through the conclusions he is forced to draw from his own, detailed studies of it. One of these examples, which Weil might well have used herself if she had been aware of it, is a hymn to the King as priest of the sun. Prevalent in the tombs and temples of Upper Egypt, it not only speaks of the divinity of the Pharaoh, but shares with the Christian faith the ideas of self-sacrifice, worship, divine judgement, justification, salvation, transfiguration, and eternal life:

Ra has appointed King N
on the earth of the living
for ever and ever;
on the day of justice for man, when the gods get satisfaction,
when the truth must out, and sins are destroyed;
he gives the gods the food of sacrifice,
dead offerings to the transfigured ones.

The name of the King N
is in heaven like (the name of) Ra (like the sun)

he lives in expansiveness of heart
like Ra Harachte (*like the sungod*)

The people exult when they see him
the folk prepare ovations for him
in his (cultic role) of the child.[27]

Far from being confined to the *Book of the Dead* or the religious writings of Plutarch, Drewermann's engagement with ancient Egyptian culture includes the Egyptian language, mythology, hymns, prayers, fairy tales, and love songs, hence much of what Father Perrin would have thought essential for a balanced account of ancient Egyptian religion. At the same time, Drewermann's reflections on the subject yield the same conclusions Weil had to draw from her own, admittedly more limited, reading of ancient texts. On the issue of divine sonship, for example, Drewermann notes:

The whole concept of the Son of God, who is born of a virgin, overshadowed by spirit and light (by Amun-Ra), born into the world was ... completely worked out in ancient Egypt as an idea thousands of years before Christianity. ... Hence we must gratefully acknowledge the fact that the theology of divine sonship was not originally developed by Christianity but borrowed from Egypt.[28]

In order to forestall any misunderstandings at this point, we should note that neither this conclusion, nor indeed Weil's perceptive remark that 'it is not for nothing that the Holy Family went down into Egypt',[29] are of merely historiographical interest – as if we could happily acknowledge the spiritual debt we owe to ancient Egypt without having to re-examine the relation between the Christian tradition and its non-Christian predecessors or contemporaries. 'Perhaps', so Weil speculates, 'at Thebes, in Egypt, God was actually present in the ram sacrificed ritually, as He is today in the consecrated host',[30] and if we recall the spirit of 'evangelical charity' revealed in Egyptian scripture, do we not have to ask why 'the Hebrews, who for four centuries were in contact with Egyptian civilization, refused to adopt this sweet spirit'?[31]

That this question is significant, not only for a proper understanding of the genealogy of Christian thought, but for a critical appraisal of the Old Testament conception of God, is brought out particularly clearly in Weil's remarks about the figure of Krishna in the Hindu scriptures, including the *Bhagavad Gita*, whose genesis can be traced back to 400 BC. Weil began to read it in the spring of 1940 and was so impressed with it – 'words with such a Christian sound, put into the mouth of an incarnation of God'[32] – that she even learnt Sanskrit and, by the summer of 1943, had begun to read the text in the original. Keen to share this spiritual discovery with others, she makes a point of drawing attention to it in her correspondence, urging her friends and family to see for themselves 'how it does one good, the language of Krishna!'[33] On hearing that her parents are bored, for example, she is incredulous. 'I can understand being unhappy,' she writes, 'but how can one be bored? Can't you think about Krishna?'[34] The well-intentioned exhortation is reiterated in subsequent letters as well,[35] and makes one wonder what it was about Krishna that prompted her continued reflections about him. Once again, her remarks on the topic are scattered across the *First and Last Notebooks*,[36] *Notebooks*,[37] and *Seventy Letters*,[38] and should be read in conjunction with the *Bhagavad Gita* itself. Three points, in particular, are worth making in this connection.

The first is the deep spiritual kinship between some of Krishna's utterances and Christ's own words in the New Testament. Consider, for example, the following remarks:

Only by love can men see me, and know me, and come unto me.[39]

The man whose love is the same for his enemies or his friends ... is dear to me.[40]

Although I am unborn, everlasting, and I am the Lord of all, I come to my realm of nature and through my wondrous power I am born.[41]

Matter is the kingdom of the earth, which in time passes away; but the Spirit is the kingdom of Light. In this body I offer sacrifice, and my body is sacrifice.[42]

In him [the Spirit supreme] all things have their life, and from him all things have come.[43]

I am the Way, and the Master who watches in silence; thy friend and thy shelter and thy abode of peace.[44]

It is not surprising that Weil should have seen in these words, uttered by a human incarnation of the one God Vishnu, and preserved in the sacred text of the *Gita*, a pre-Christian analogue of God's revelation through Jesus and the New Testament. It might be argued that, in spite of these ostensible similarities, we cannot really tell how far the analogy may be carried until we have compared the distinctly *Christian* conception of love with that which allows a Hindu believer to 'come unto' Krishna. This is true.[45] On the other hand – and this seems to be Weil's question as well – can we legislate in advance that, since Christianity claims to be the one and only true religion, Krishna's conception of love, including love of one's neighbour, *must* have been inferior to that proclaimed by Christ in the Sermon on the Mount and elsewhere in the New Testament?

Admittedly, the Krishna stories, unlike the story of Christ in the Gospels, have a genealogy in which aspects of much older mythical and historical figures are eventually fused with the person of Krishna Vasudeva, founder of the monotheistic religion of the Bhagavata (Sanskrit: 'One devoted to Bhagavat (Lord)') in 200 BC, but none of this prehistory undermines what is spiritually important about Krishna, viz. that he was not merely a mythological construct, but a living embodiment of perfect righteousness; that the *Gita* celebrates his life as an incarnation of Vishnu, the one God who brings life to all who follow him; and that his pronouncements are often profoundly Christian in orientation.

The second point concerns the Hindu believer's tolerance towards the followers of other faiths. When Krishna insists that 'even those who in faith worship other gods, because of their love, they worship me, although not in the right way',[46] we are reminded of Vatican II and its similarly charitable document *Lumen Gentium* (1964), according to which

> those also can attain eternal salvation who without fault on their part do not know the Gospel of Christ and His Church, but seek God with a sincere heart, and under the influence of grace endeavour to do His will as recognized through the promptings of their conscience.[47]

Unfortunately, Krishna's remark also recalls the Catholic Church's earlier position on the issue of salvation, such as it was proclaimed by Boniface VIII in his Bull *Unam sanctam* (1302), for instance:

There is only one, holy, catholic and apostolic Church we are compelled by faith to believe and hold, and we firmly believe in her and sincerely confess her, outside of whom there is neither salvation nor remission of sins...[48]

Weil would no doubt have applauded *Lumen Gentium* for its inclusive tone *vis-à-vis* other religious faiths, but she would also have wondered why it has taken the Church so long to recognise the wisdom of Krishna's gesture.

This leads us to the third point worth noting in connection with the *Bhagavad Gita*. Among other things, it tells us of an imminent battle between the Pandavas and the Kauravas, and Krishna's refusal to bear arms. Instead, Krishna offers the opposing parties a choice between his personal presence and the loan of his army. The Pandavas, including Krishna's disciple Arjuna, choose the former, and the Kauravas the latter. Weil sees in the choice 'an ordeal' which 'indicates infallibly the lawful side and the unlawful side',[49] the difference between good and evil, as well as a symbolic representation of man's existential predicament: 'God gives himself to Man under the aspect of power or under that of perfection: the choice is left to Man. [Krishna's army – is it not the Prince of this World?]'[50] It is precisely this Christian gesture of *renunciation* (of power, worldly good, self-interest, etc.) that makes Krishna a prefiguration of Christ, and turns his pronouncements into the Word of God. But Krishna's disciple Arjuna, too, displays the wisdom of divine counsel, not only by choosing Krishna as charioteer – and hence as *servant* – but in his understanding of what it means to engage in battle with his fellow-men:

Facing us in the field of battle are teachers, fathers, and sons; grandsons, grandfathers, wives' brothers; mothers' brothers and fathers of wives. ... These I do not wish to slay, even if I myself am slain. Not even for the kingdom of the three worlds: how much less for a kingdom of the earth. ... Even if they, with minds overcome by greed, see no evil in the destruction of a family, see no sin in the treachery to friends; ... Shall we not, who see the evil of destruction, shall we not refrain from this terrible deed?[51]

Weil does not quote this passage in her own work, nor does she draw an explicit analogy between the *Gita*'s reflections on the terribleness of war and Homer's insights into the warriors' predicament in the *Iliad*, but her comments on the latter suggest that Arjuna's remarks come surprisingly close to the spirit of Homer's narrative:

> So the idea was born of a destiny beneath which the aggressors and their victims are equally innocent, the victors and the vanquished brothers in the same misfortune. The vanquished is a cause of misfortune for the victor as much as the victor is for the vanquished.[52]

Weil illustrates this remark with this quotation from the *Iliad:*

> An only son is born to him, for a short life; moreover
> He grows old abandoned by me, since far from home
> I linger before Troy, doing harm to you and to your sons.[53]

For Weil, the point of drawing attention to what the *Gita* and the *Iliad* have to teach us about our common humanity is to make us aware, not only of Indian and Greek spirituality, but of the contrast between those spiritualities and the attitude of the Hebrews depicted in the Old Testament writings. As Weil puts it:

> The Hebrews ... saw their vanquished as an abomination in God's sight and therefore condemned to expiate their crimes. Thus cruelty was sanctioned and even inevitable. Nor does any text of the Old Testament sound a note comparable to that of the Greek epic, unless perhaps certain parts of the poem of Job. The Romans and Hebrews have been admired, read, imitated in actions and in words, cited every time there was need to justify a crime, throughout twenty centuries of Christianity.[54]

In the first volume of her *Notebooks*, Weil assembles a long catalogue of Old Testament atrocities which condemn both its perpetrators and the 'divine' will that supposedly informed their decision to carry them out.[55] This 'tissue of horrors'[56] includes God's commands that the Levites massacre brothers, friends, and parents (Exodus 32.27–8); that Saul 'completely destroy the entire Amalekite nation – men, women, children, babies, cattle, sheep, camels, and donkeys' (1 Sam 15.3); that the Israelites completely annihilate the Hittites, Amorites, Canaanites, Perizzites, Hivites, and Jebusites (Deuteronomy 20.15–18); that a man be put to death because he had gathered sticks on a Sabbath (Numbers 15.32–6);

and the fact that Joshua can make the sun stand still, just 'so as to have more time to wipe out the vanquished' (Joshua 10.13).[57] It strikes Weil that, whenever such gross acts of violence are committed in the name of God, they already constitute a perversion, an idolatrous conception, of the very notion of divine command, and if she ranks the spiritual value of the *Bhagavad Gita* so highly, it is because of Krishna's declamation that 'the man who is born for heaven' must subscribe to 'non-violence, truth, freedom from anger, renunciation, serenity, aversion to fault-finding, sympathy for all beings, peace from greedy cravings, gentleness, modesty' and a host of other Christian virtues.[58]

Weil's own explanation of what motivated the Hebrews of the Old Testament to act as they did is that their self-deceiving adoration of earthly power caused them to lose their grip on the distinction between right and wrong. 'The worship of power caused the Hebrews to lose the idea of good and evil', she writes to Jean Wahl in 1941, at the same time confessing that she has 'always been kept away from Christianity by its ranking these stories, so full of pitiless cruelty, as sacred texts'.[59] Weil, never afraid to say what she thinks, is aware that the implications of this confession will mark her out as a 'heretic', and prevent her from joining the very church to which she has always felt the deepest spiritual attachment. One implication of her comparative religious studies is that the majority of writings composing the Old Testament is, in fact, unworthy of being included in the canon, indeed *any* canon, of sacred texts:

> Among all the books of the Old Testament, only a small number (Isaiah, Job, the Song of Solomon, Daniel, Tobias, part of Ezekiel, part of the Psalms, part of the Books of Wisdom, the beginning of Genesis ...) are able to be assimilated by a Christian soul, together with a few principles scattered here and there throughout the others.[60]

Another implication, closely connected with the first, is that there are serious intellectual and spiritual obstacles – and we need to remember that, for Weil, the notion of the spiritual is always tied to that of perfect goodness – to identifying the God of the New Testament with that of the Old:

> I have never been able to understand how it is possible for a reasonable mind to regard the Jehovah of the Bible and the Father who is invoked in the Gospel as one and the same being.[61]

Indeed, Weil identifies the influence of the Old Testament as a major reason for the corruption of Christianity,[62] and concludes that 'among all the characters in the Old Testament accounts, Daniel's is the only pure one (apart from Abel, Enoch, Noah, Melchizedek and Job)'.[63] Weil's views on the Old Testament, not unlike those of the ancient Roman heretic Marcion, are bound to provoke outrage, especially among orthodox Christians. However, if one considers the spiritual repository of non-Christian religions and accepts Christ's teaching as the paradigm of the Good, against which alone all things spiritual must be measured, is one not entitled to ask on what grounds, other than dogmatic stipulation, one can insist that the pictures of God and piety drawn in the majority of the Old Testament writings *must be* superior to, or deeper than, those enshrined in the sacred writings of other cultures?

But perhaps the question is as hasty as Weil's condemnation of the texts in question. Certainly, passages like Deuteronomy 7.1–2, in which God commands the Israelites to destroy all the inhabitants of the land they are about to conquer, present serious interpretative difficulties. 'If we take the text in its straightforward meaning,' so Gareth Moore rightly notes, 'the passage is indeed horrible and certainly incompatible with Christian principles'.[64] On the other hand, there might be good reasons for adopting a 'spiritualised' reading of the text, as biblical scholars like John Barton have proposed.[65] On Barton's view, the authors of Deuteronomy, far from endorsing the command of genocide – which would, in any case, have been unknown at the time of the conquest – are merely taking it as a symbol of religious transformation, and hence in a sense that is diametrically opposed to the surface meaning of the text.[66]

Gareth Moore also agrees that 'if it is possible to read it with integrity as a call to religious reformation ... then there is no reason why authentic religious believers must disown it'[67] and expunge it from the canon of Old Testament writings. Whether such reinterpretations could plausibly be provided for all, or even most, of the other Old Testament passages to which Weil objects in her *Notebooks*, could only be decided after careful exegetical engagement with the text itself. But, as Moore and Barton have pointed out, it would be more than uncharitable to charge the authors of the Old Testament with spiritual blindness when there are interpretative possibilities that Simone Weil failed to see herself. In this connection, we should also recall Father Perrin's puzzlement about Weil's reading of the Old Testament:

Why does Simone forget that the revelation of God and of creation was vouchsafed to Israel? That it was given to Moses to formulate the Great Commandment? Why does she pass over in silence the fact that the Old Testament was unique in forbidding human sacrifices? Why does she not quote the admirable injunctions concerning pity for the stranger, the needy ... even to the goat which must not be cooked in its mother's milk?[68]

It is interesting to note that the kinds of interpretative difficulties raised in connection with the Old Testament also apply to the *Bhagavad Gita*. Attentive readers of this ancient text will be quick to point out that even Krishna tells his disciple Arjuna that 'there is no greater good for a warrior than to fight in righteous war', and that he should arise, therefore, 'with soul ready to fight',[69] which suggests that Krishna is not all that different from the God of the Israelites, after all. However, as Juan Mascaró insists in his introduction to the *Gita*, the war imagery calls for a spiritual reading of the text, not for a literal-historical interpretation.[70] 'Be a warrior and kill desire, the powerful enemy of the soul',[71] Krishna proclaims, and the sword which he wants Arjuna to take up is 'the sword of wisdom' in a battle whose object is the liberation of his own soul from the 'enemies' of goodness and love.[72]

Paying close attention to the spiritual meaning of the *Bhagavad Gita*, one can see that its underlying motif is not the quest for earthly power or the desire to subjugate through physical force, but precisely the opposite: the *renunciation* of such power in favour of the transcendent power of divine *love*. As Jesus said to Pilate: 'My kingdom is not of this world: if my kingdom were of this world, then would my servants fight, that I should not be delivered to the Jews: but now is my kingdom not from hence.'[73] For Weil, the significance of Christ's remark for our understanding of God could not have been anticipated more clearly than in the *Gita*'s depiction of Krishna's renunciatory gesture: 'God here below cannot be anything else but absolutely powerless. ... It is necessary that Krishna should be separated from his army, that he should only take part in the battle as a charioteer, as a servant.'[74]

We have now reached a point in the discussion where many readers are likely to object that, even if we agree with Weil that Christ's incarnation may have been preceded by others – e.g. Noah, Melchizedek, Osiris, Krishna, etc. – it is still obscure how such incarnations would have to be understood. For if talk of divine incarnations is, as Weil rightly insists, more than a *metaphorical* way of talking about a particular historical individual's moral integrity, then it seems that we have to construe such talk *literally*, and it is wholly unclear what *that* would mean. Some of Weil's commentators prefer to speak of 'the historical incarnation' instead, but seem to be in disagreement over the importance Weil attached to it, even in regard to Christ. Thus, Patricia Little writes:

> Simone Weil's interpretation pays little heed to the historicity or otherwise of these various traditions. It is perhaps because the historicity of Christ himself was not of central concern to her that she is able to assimilate him so easily to similar figures. She did not deny the historical incarnation ... but she never gives the impression that it is of great importance.[75]

Jean-Marie Perrin, on the other hand, is adamant that, even though there are occasions when Weil 'seem[s] to be slipping into syncretism', i.e. fusing diverse religious beliefs and practices that should be kept separate,

> it must not be forgotten that she eagerly affirms the historical reality of the Incarnation and of the life of Our Lord and that if she searches for traces of him in all places it is because she wants to bring all things to him.[76]

Now, it is true that Weil's speculations about previous incarnations always take Christ as their spiritual reference point and paradigm, and that she sees Christ's incarnation as a kind of consummation – in her *Notebooks*, for instance, she asks herself: 'If Krishna himself were troubled in spirit, as Christ was in the Gospel, wouldn't it be far more beautiful?'[77] However, it does not follow from this that Weil would accept the terms in which commentators have couched the problem, or that she should be able to elaborate on *how*, exactly, God can become incarnated in man. What she wants us to see is that the Incarnation is just as *unintelligible* as the reality of grace and Christ's presence in the Eucharist, and that its spiritual hold on us is intimately connected with its being an unfathomable *mystery*. Like grace and the Eucharist, the Incarnation is nothing other than

> [e]ternity which descends to insert itself into time. Incarnation represents the maximum of such insertion. Relations between man and God, between time and eternity, between the relative

and the absolute, are in any case unintelligible. There is no degree of unintelligibility; everything on this subject is as unintelligible as the Eucharist.[78]

Weil goes on to elaborate on this remark by noting that there can be no *historical* proof of the Incarnation, nothing that would count as confirmatory 'evidence' in the ordinary sense of the word, and that, if one wants to talk of 'proof' at all, there can be 'one only: the internal evidence contained in the text lying in front of us'.[79] What lends authority to the belief in Jesus' divinity, in other words, is the *content* of the scriptural tradition surrounding his life and work, and not some independent, external justification. Indeed, to ask for the latter would be equivalent to demanding *physical* evidence for a *metaphysical* phenomenon, and thus an absurdity. In her *Letter to a Priest*, Weil illustrates this point with a helpful example:

The propositions 'Jesus Christ is God' or 'The consecrated bread and wine are the body and blood of Christ', enunciated as facts, have strictly speaking no meaning whatever. The value of these propositions is totally different from the truth contained in the correct enunciation of a fact (for example: Salazar is head of the Portuguese Government) or of a geometrical theorem. This value does not strictly speaking belong to the order of truth, but to a higher order; for it is a value impossible for the intelligence to grasp, except indirectly, through the effects produced. And truth, in the strict sense, belongs to the domain of the intelligence.[80]

It was a *fact* that Jesus' cross bore the inscription 'I.N.R.I' (Jesus of Nazareth, King of the Jews), and one that could easily have been demonstrated to those who doubted it – 'Just look and see for yourself!' – whereas a sentence like 'Jesus is the Christ', is of a completely different order and, as Weil rightly says, 'impossible for the intelligence to grasp'. When the penitent thief who was hanging with Jesus rebuked the other criminal by telling him that 'this man [Jesus] has done nothing wrong', and when he asked Jesus to 'remember me when you come into your kingdom',[81] he did so because he saw God in Jesus, but of course this 'seeing' was nothing like his seeing 'I.N.R.I.' inscribed on Jesus' cross. If the penitent thief hadn't been sure that the man beside him was innocent, he would hardly have been able to dispel his doubt by taking a closer look at him, analogously to the way in which he might have strained his eyes to get a clearer view of what was actually happening on the ground beneath him. Similarly for the recognition of Jesus as the Son of God. Weil, who is closely following Kant's thinking here, reminds us that 'fact belongs to the domain of time' and that 'the domain of reality extends infinitely beyond that of fact',[82] with the consequence that we can speak of Jesus' divinity as *real*, without having to invoke the notion of a *fact*.

This is not merely a verbal matter, but an important observation about the nature of religious belief. Returning for a moment to the penitent thief, it is clear that his unfaltering belief in God is itself a matter of *grace* – as much, in fact, as the remorse he feels for his own criminal actions. His realisation that he has done wrong and his acknowledgement of Jesus' innocence go hand in hand, and what is remarkable about his exchange with Jesus is not only that the thief, unlike the apostle Peter at the time of Jesus' interrogation by the Sanhedrin, does see God in Jesus, but that he should do so at the darkest moment of Jesus' earthly life. Weil sees in the thief's attitude towards Jesus a miraculous *reading* of the latter's divinity, as well as a powerful representation of our dependence on God's grace when it comes to our own reading of the world.[83] 'Who is able to flatter himself that he is able to read correctly?', Weil asks, and the allusion to Peter's self-assured promises – 'Lord, with you I am ready to go even to prison and death'[84] – is evident.

However, our dependence on God's grace extends well beyond the domain of personal hopes and aspirations, to include even the continued existence of Christianity itself. It is tempting to think that, since the powers of evil have not *prevailed* thus far, the grace of God *will* ensure that Christianity, for example, continues indefinitely into the future. If Simone Weil is far more cautious about such predictions, it is not least because of what she takes *grace* to be: a wholly undeserved gift from God, neither granted nor withheld in accordance with human expectations. In spite of various corrupting influences on the Church, Weil argues,

the text of the Gospel, the Lord's Prayer, and the sacraments still retain their redemptive power. It is only in this sense that hell has not prevailed. The word of Christ guarantees nothing more than this, and in particular it in no way guarantees perpetuity for Christianity. (If Christianity disappeared, would it be followed in a few centuries' time by another religion, and would that religion arise from a new incarnation?)[85]

Elsewhere, Weil even goes so far as to wonder what might happen 'if the Catholic Church were to be destroyed' – perhaps people would come to believe one day that Jesus, the Word, and the Son were all different Gods?[86] With this remark, we are returned once more to the issue of the *uniqueness* of the Incarnation, and to Weil's suggestion that this uniqueness must be sought, not in the number of its manifestations, but in its spiritual content. As D. Z. Phillips has put it:

> If [Weil] insists that *the same* truths she finds in Christianity are found elsewhere, why does that fact make the truths any less unique? Could we not speak of *the same* incarnate truth in the different contexts?[87]

These are precisely the kinds of questions that occupied Weil's mind during the latter years of her life. Deeply disenchanted with the spiritual narrowness and exclusiveness revealed in certain Christian and Hebraic traditions, she felt the need to meditate on the concept of the Incarnation more deeply and without intellectual condescension to the illumination provided by other religious traditions. No matter how vigorously we may wish to applaud or criticise the results of her meditations, we must not forget what she told Father Perrin just before she left for New York: 'In the domain of holy things', she assured him, 'I affirm nothing categorically.'[88]

If one were asked to describe Weil's spiritual development thus far, one would have to say that she came to God, to a deeper understanding of who he is, not through philosophical or other kinds of argument, but through her meditation on Christ and his Passion. In this connection, her spiritual epiphany in 1938 plays an important role and should not go unmentioned, even though Weil herself was reluctant to talk about it, not only because the experience was intensely personal and too ephemeral to be expressed in words, but because of her more general conviction that 'to try to express the inexpressible is to degrade it'.[89] As noted in Chapter 1, all she tells us is that, 'at the moment when Christ came to take possession of me for the first time', she was reciting her favourite poem, George Herbert's 'Love', and that she felt 'a presence more personal, more certain, and more real than that of a human being'.[90] From that moment onwards, many things in her life assume a different aspect: the poem now strikes her as if it had always been a prayer; God and Christ become 'irresistibly mingled' in her thoughts; Homer's *Iliad* seems 'bathed in Christian light', and Plato appears as a mystic,[91] even though she has never read any of the mystics, because, as she herself confesses, 'I had never felt any call to read them.'[92]

Indeed, in a subsequent letter to her brother André she even wonders whether one should attempt to articulate and study mystical experiences at all:

> It is possible that in the earlier period the Greeks voluntarily abstained from such studies, believing that there are some things which ought not to be formulated and extending this obligation of secrecy, in certain matters, even to the soul's dialogue with itself. In parenthesis, if they did so believe I think they were quite right; I admire St. Teresa but I think she would be even more admirable if she had never written. But that they knew states of ecstasy and set a high value on them there can be no doubt. The writings of Plato are a sufficient witness.[93]

Could it not be that God had prevented her from coming into contact with mystical literature, 'so that it should be evident to me that I had not invented this absolutely unexpected contact'?[94] Her concern is that, since we have a natural tendency to project our deepest hopes and expectations into our future experiences, and since certain kinds of literature serve to reinforce that tendency, there is always a danger that, through autosuggestion and other such mechanisms, we come to mistake for reality what is, in fact, merely the product of our own imagination. Such delusional episodes are, of course, particularly significant if they concern spiritual matters, hence the need, acknowledged even by such venerable mystics as Teresa of Avila and St John of the Cross, for vigilant self-criticism and self-reflection.[95] It was because Weil was permanently on guard against the possibility of self-deception that she could assure her friend Joë Bousquet that her thoughts on these matters expressed more than her own, subjective opinion:

> I would never dare to speak to you like this if all these thoughts were the product of my own mind. ... I do really have the feeling, in spite of myself, that God is addressing all this to you, through me.[96]

Given that Weil came to know God through her experience of, and subsequent meditation on, Christ, we must now ask how all this influenced her thinking about related concepts, including God's creation, the existence of evil and affliction, the nature and role of the Church, her own vocation, belief in miracles, and the hope for eternal life. As the above quotation shows, Weil could not help thinking of herself – with all due humility – as an instrument or messenger of God's Word, so these issues need to be explored in more detail.

7

Religious Reflection (3): Creation, Affliction, and Last Things

It is a central feature of Weil's understanding of God that 'not only the Passion but the Creation itself is a renunciation and sacrifice on the part of God. The Passion is simply its consummation.'[1] Indeed, one could say that the entire narrative of God's self-disclosure to man, from the creation to the Incarnation and Passion of Christ, revolves around the two interconnected themes of *renunciation* and *love*:

> His love maintains in existence, in a free and autonomous exis-
> tence, beings other than himself, beings other than the good,
> mediocre beings. Through love, he abandons them to affliction
> and sin. For if he did not abandon them they would not exist.
> His presence would annul their existence as a flame kills a
> butterfly.[2]

Initially, this view of God's relation to his creation sounds highly paradoxical. How could a loving God abandon us to affliction and allow us to commit sinful deeds? But we must be careful not to anthropomorphise God. His abandonment is *not* what it would be if he were a human being. The apostle Peter abandoned Jesus when he denied knowing him, just as the captain of a ship may abandon the passengers in his care, or a mother her child, and we rightly think that such actions are deeply reprehensible. God's abandonment of human beings, on the other hand, is not of that kind. As we saw in connection with Weil's comments on the essentially paradoxical character of the belief in God's reality, his absence is the very *condition* of our existence, and should therefore be taken as a manifestation of his infinite *love*. 'The World', Weil writes, 'is God's language to us' and the only bridge to God, though it is also a necessary veil that allows God to remain unsullied by our sinfulness and imperfection.[3] Weil captures this thought in an illuminating analogy:

> Let us imagine two prisoners, in neighbouring cells, who communicate by means of taps on the wall. The wall is what separates them, but it is also what enables them to communicate. It is the same with God. Every separation represents a bond.[4]

The 'wall' between us and God is the entire physical universe, infinitely extended in space and time and therefore infinitely 'thick', as it were, and yet God communicates himself to us through all kinds of spiritual 'taps', asking us to respond to him in turn, e.g. through worship, prayer, and doing his will. Given that 'we are as mediocre and as far from God as it is possible for creatures endowed with reason to be', it follows that the distance to be crossed by both God and his creatures is infinite, and that the only path to God is the very love from which his creation emanated in the first place:

> It was by an inconceivable love that God created beings so distant from himself. It is by an inconceivable love that he comes down so far as to reach them. It is by an inconceivable love that they then ascend so far as to reach him.[5]

Now God's omnipotence is frequently thought of as an (infinite) extension of earthly power, and the Creation narrative as an illustration of that power, but we can already see from the above quotations that Weil would consider this reading both idolatrous and superficial: idolatrous in its anthropomorphic conception of power, and superficial in its elucidation of the spiritual significance of the Creation story. If the latter is read analogously to Christ's Passion, however, then its central theme is no longer an impressive display of divine power, but a sacrificial act in which such power is, in fact, renounced or, what amounts to the same thing, an act in which God's power is revealed to *be* the power of love. It is hard to read the story of God's creation differently, once Christ's self-sacrifice in the Passion is seen as a perfect reflection of the Father's own nature. Indeed, doesn't the doctrine of the Trinity proclaim precisely this essential unity of Son and Father in the one God?

For Weil, the proper human response to God's self-renunciation in the Creation is also clear: it can only be our own *de-creation*, effected by a radical detachment from that part of our natures which pulls us towards sin and degradation, and hence away from God: 'In a sense God renounces being everything. We should renounce being something. That is our only good.'[6] If God, out of love, allows such imperfect creatures as ourselves to exist at all, the appropriate response to his renunciatory gesture is to lessen that imperfection within ourselves, so that we move with our whole being towards the very state of perfection that God sacrificed for us in the first place. Weil writes: 'Through grace, the individual "I" can decreate itself, the "I" little by little disappears, and God loves himself by way of the creature, which empties itself, and becomes nothing.'[7] The suggestion that 'God loves himself' initially sounds strange and seems quite incompatible with the belief that God has created the universe because he loves us, but Weil thinks that the matter is not as straightforward as that. Strictly speaking, God can only love that which is perfectly good, viz. himself, and not creatures, who are, after all, *infinitely* less perfect than he is. We are not really worthy of God's love, then, except in so far as we have been created in his image and are capable of orientating ourselves towards holiness when grace comes to our aid. But God can love himself *through* us, if we give ourselves up to him and, paradoxical though it may seem, offer him in return the very existence that we have received from him:

> Creation is an act of love and it is perpetual. At each moment our existence is God's love for us. But God can only love himself. His love for us is love for himself through us. Thus, he who gives us our being loves in us the acceptance of not being. Our existence is made up only of his waiting for our acceptance not to exist. He is perpetually begging from us that existence which he gives. He gives it to us in order to beg it from us.[8]

If this is the right way to look on our existence, then, as Weil herself asks, 'in what sense is it a good that I should exist, and not

God alone?' In response, she can only confess that she does not know, and of course her silence on this point is just as appropriate as it would be if someone asked her why this world exists at all.[9] It is a mystery in which all questions come to a end. What we *can* say, however, is that the central key to understanding God's creation is the very idea of *renunciation* that, according to Weil, also informs the Passion of Christ, the Stoicism of Marcus Aurelius, the spirit of poverty manifested in St Francis of Assisi, and the self-effacement of all those who genuinely love their neighbours.

But how far should our 'de-creation' go? Weil says: 'To see a landscape such as it is when I am not there. When I am anywhere, I pollute the silence of earth and sky with my breathing and the beating of my heart.' [10] Does my presence in a breathtakingly beautiful landscape already constitute a stain on the beauty of God's creation, such that it were better if I was not there at all? Is Christ the only one whose presence did not sully that beauty because his eyes, unlike ours, were not those of a fallen sinner? Is the extent of our depravity such that we should join Weil in exclaiming, 'I should joyfully obey the order to go to the very centre of hell and to remain there eternally'?[11] It is true that the boundary between humility and self-loathing is easily crossed, and it is tempting to reproach Weil for indulging in the kind of spiritual self-flagellation that is merely a disguised form of ingratitude for life. But we do not have to read her remarks that way, and Weil herself was too astute a thinker not to sense in advance the effect her thoughts might have on others. This is why she tries to forestall possible misunderstandings by telling Father Perrin:

> I hope though that in owning my wretchedness to you I did not give you the impression of misunderstanding God's mercy. I hope I have never fallen, and never shall fall, to such a depth of cowardice and ingratitude.[12]

The point of Weil's remark about joyfully accepting the order to go to hell, too, is not to incite universal self-loathing, but to draw attention to the notion of *obedience* in relation to God's will, and to instil in the reader a proper regard for God's radical otherness, a sense of humility. Hence Weil's rejoinder: 'I do not mean, of course, that I have a preference for orders of this nature. I am not perverse like that.'[13] Nor, we might add, would such a 'perverse' view of human existence sit easily with the belief that man has been created in God's image, as a product of infinite love.

123

And the existence of evil in the world? How is *that* to be reconciled with a loving God? Even if we accept that God has created us as free and autonomous beings, who are the sole authors of much of the evil that befalls them, are there not still a host of natural evils which it would be 'perverse' to see under the aspect of love? Consider R. S. Thomas's poem 'The Island':

And God said, I will build a church here
And cause this people to worship me,
And afflict them with poverty and sickness
In return for centuries of hard work
And patience. And its walls shall be hard as
Their hearts, and its windows let in the light
Grudgingly, as their minds do, and the priest's words be
    drowned
By the winds caterwauling. All this I will do,

Said God, and watch the bitterness in their eyes
Grow, and their lips suppurate with
Their prayers. And their women shall bring forth
On my altars, and I will choose the best
Of them to be thrown back into the sea.
And that was only on one island.[14]

Weil's reaction to this poem would, I think, have three aspects. First, she would agree that such terrible misfortunes as poverty, sickness, and death at sea must not be brushed aside as unfortunate side-effects of God's creative act, since that would belittle the suffering they involve. Second, she would strongly oppose any attempt to justify such evils, be it in terms of some earthly good that outweighs them, or in terms of a 'higher' good known only to God. One only needs to recall the recent tsunami catastrophe to see how repugnant it would be to speak of a 'justification' in this context. Weil writes:

We must not try to reduce evil to good by seeking compensations or justifications for evil. We must love God through the evil that occurs, solely because everything that actually occurs is real and behind all reality stands God.[15]

This does not mean that we should *love* evil – which would not only be perverse but idolatrous – but that we must love God *through* the evil.[16] For Weil, the evil is 'a sign of the distance between us and God', and, if you recall our earlier discussion of God's necessary absence, 'this distance is love and therefore should be loved'.[17] In other words, we should recognise that evil and affliction are aspects of the very same tissue of necessities that separates us from God; that we must *want* God to be separated from us because 'without the protection of space, time, and of matter, we should be evaporated like water in the sun';[18] and that 'God does not send sufferings and woes as ordeals; he lets Necessity distribute them in accordance with its own proper mechanism'.[19]

We have already noted that, for Weil, the concepts of *order* and *beauty* are closely connected, indeed that the perception of order is a precondition of all genuine experiences of beauty. In the notion of *necessity*, which is the third facet of Weil's response to evil and affliction, both concepts are fused with that of divine love, so that the entire universe now appears under the aspects of (divine) love, order, and beauty, even when our individual experiences are painful rather than joyous. Again, this does not mean that a terrible affliction is a good thing, let alone beautiful, but that it is possible for a faithful believer to see *through* the tissue of necessities with which his experiences are bound up, and to see something of God's love and beauty even in his own suffering. And isn't this precisely the vision that was granted to the penitent thief on the cross? And doesn't the demeanour of Christ himself show that even the most tortured, degraded, and despised creature can yet continue to love with that part of his soul over which affliction has no power?[20] This reading also informs Weil's understanding of Christ's words on the cross, 'Eloi, Eloi, lamma Sabbacthani?' (Matthew 27.46):

> The only part of our soul which is not a fit subject for affliction is the part which is situated in the other world. Affliction has no power over it – for perhaps, as Meister Eckhart says, it is uncreated – but it has the power to sever it violently from the temporal part of the soul, so that, although supernatural love dwells in the soul, its sweetness is not felt. It is then that the cry breaks out: 'My God, why hast thou forsaken me?'[21]

While it is true that Christ's suffering was inflicted by men, rather than by natural causes, he nevertheless submitted to God's will with perfect obedience, similarly to the way in which a sailor submits to the necessities that constitute the motion of the waves. This is why Weil, if she had been able to read R. S. Thomas's 'The Island', would have responded to it with this remark from her essay 'The Love of God and Affliction':

> The sea is not less beautiful in our eyes because we know that sometimes ships are wrecked by it. On the contrary, this adds to its beauty. If it altered the movement of its waves to spare a boat, it would be a creature gifted with discernment and choice and not this fluid, perfectly obedient to every external pressure. It is this perfect obedience that constitutes the sea's beauty.[22]

Weil's suggestion that natural necessities should be conceived under the aspects of order, beauty, and love, and seen as an image of *obedience*, not only adds an important dimension to her insights into the relation between God and the universe, but to our understanding of the expression 'Thy will be done' from the Lord's Prayer. It makes us aware of the fact that God's will extends far beyond the domain of human concerns and interests, and that there is a sense in which his response to our supplications is already contained in the tissue of necessities within which our lives must necessarily unfold.

There is a temptation, epitomised in the story of Job, to wonder why these necessities are not more favourable to our needs and desires, why God's will could not have been more amenable to our own. Weil would resist this (natural) temptation, and point out that she is not offering us a philosophical or theological *argument* in support of the conviction that the cross is the only path to God. Rather, she is trying to bring us into a spiritual perspective from which we can see why 'all the horrors produced in this world are like the folds imposed upon the waves by gravity',[23] and why even 'those whom we call criminals are only tiles blown off a roof by the wind and falling at random'.[24] This is not to exculpate the wrongdoer – he *did*, as Weil admits, become a criminal by his initial choice – or to minimise the evil done – even Christ's glorified body bore the marks of his wounds – but to remember Christ's compassionate plea that his tormentors may be forgiven (Luke 23.34), as they are ignorant of the true meaning of what they are doing. Every flight from divine love involves such ignorance, and a surrender to the psychological forces that bind the 'I' to this world:

> When ... a man turns away from God, he simply gives himself up to the law of gravity. Then he thinks that he can decide and choose, but he is only a thing, a stone that falls.[25]

Such gravity can be overcome with the help of grace, however, and this is something for which we must pray.

Once we have come to embrace the picture Weil has unfolded here, we also see that the kinds of philosophico-theological contortions through which many contemporary philosophers of religion go in order to reconcile God's benevolence with the existence of evil and suffering are misguided and should be abandoned for a perspective in which love and beauty lie at the centre. Viewed through these lenses,

> relentless necessity, misery, distress, the crushing burden of poverty and of exhausting labour, cruelty, torture, violent death, constraint, terror, disease – all this is but the divine love. It is God who out of love withdraws from us so that we can love him.[26]

Weil's vocation, baptism, and the Church

Before we turn to Weil's relation to the Church, the nature of her spiritual vocation, and the reasons for her refusal to be baptised, we should comment on her highly critical attitude towards Israel and the associated idea of a chosen people. It is worth noting, in this context, that the 1947 French edition of *Gravity and Grace* contained a chapter entitled 'Israel', which was subsequently excised from the English, German, and other translations, and has only recently (2002) been included again.[27] Admittedly, Weil's remarks on Israel's role in the development of Christianity are unusually dismissive, not to say indignant, in tone. She writes, for example, that

> the curse of Israel rests on Christendom. Israel meant atrocities, the Inquisition, the extermination of heretics and infidels. Israel meant (and to a certain extent still does ...) capitalism. Israel means totalitarianism, especially with regard to its worst enemies.[28]

Elsewhere in the chapter, she likens Israel's God to the 'temporal sovereign' of the Romans, 'on a par with the Emperor',[29] and argues that 'this is how the birth of Christianity was marked with the Roman stain before it became the official religion of the Empire'.[30] Not a few commentators have seen in these and Weil's other remarks on Judaism 'an insupportable outrage',[31] and accused her of being an 'enem[y] of Jewish humanity'.[32] Even Gustave Thibon speaks of Weil's 'passionate anti-semitism',[33] though he knew better than anyone that Weil was as far removed from Nazism as Himmler was from being a Catholic. That he nevertheless describes her attitude as 'anti-semitism' instead suggests that he understood something about Weil's deep reservations about Old Testament spirituality, and was aware of the kinds of consideration that prompted her to reject the Hebraic God as 'a carnal and collective God', who seemed to have so little in common with the 'absent' God of Christ.[34]

In the light of our earlier discussion of this issue, it is easy to see why Weil would equally reject the idea of a *chosen* people, understood as a people who have entered into a contractual agreement with a divinity whose promises are 'purely temporal', rather than eternal.[35] Dewi Phillips puts the point well in *The Problem of Evil and the Problem of God*:

> To be a servant of God ... is to want to love God. That love is not of this world. That is precisely why it may be called upon to suffer in the world. The sacrifice of worldliness may be called on to suffer by the world, precisely because of its reaction to such sacrifice. It is not that God first chooses a people and then, for reasons best known to himself, makes them suffer. Rather, it is *when* people suffer for God, *when* their love of God brings suffering on them, that they are God's chosen people. This is not a bestowal of grace or a calling at any particular time, but the terms of an eternal covenant that reveals what it is to serve God *at any time*.[36]

Weil on the threshold

In the light of Weil's intense engagement with the Christian faith and her conviction that it constituted 'the only possible' attitude towards life, and in view of the strong attraction she felt towards the Catholic faith, in particular, one wonders why she remained on the threshold of the Church and persistently refused to be baptised. The reasons, as she explains in the 35 'heretical' theses of her *Letter to a Priest* (1942), are manifold, but the following considerations played a particularly important role in her decision to remain outside institutionalised religion. The first, expressed most succinctly in a letter to Jean Wahl, concerns various *philosophical* misgivings in relation to Church dogma:

I adhere totally to the mysteries of the Christian faith, with the only kind of adherence which seems to me appropriate for mysteries. This adherence is love, not affirmation. Certainly I belong to Christ – or so I hope and believe. But I am kept outside the Church by philosophical difficulties which I fear are irreducible. They do not concern the mysteries themselves but the accretions of definition with which the Church has seen fit to clothe them in the course of centuries; and above all the use in this connection of the words *anathema sit*.[37]

Even her closest Catholic friends in Marseilles had already wondered whether Weil might have joined the Church more readily if she hadn't enjoyed such an extensive training in philosophy. Thus, Father Perrin laments that 'in Simone Weil the conflict between the certitude of religious experience and her philosophical mentality went very deep',[38] and that 'she had difficulty on account of a certain rationalism which the great discovery of Christ had not removed'.[39] Gustave Thibon, too, finds in her refusal to be baptised 'the sign of a deep interior separation' between her desire for full participation in the sacraments, and 'an intellectual rigidity' which prompted her to throw into question anything her conscience could not accept.[40] In response to Weil's reservations, Thibon writes:

A great many Catholics, born in the Church, nourished by its sap and bathed in its atmosphere, have never thought of asking themselves whether they adhere with all their mind to the articles of the Council of Trent. Often they do not even know them.[41]

Thibon may well be right in saying that most Roman Catholic believers have never read a single line of the Council of Trent's pronouncements, and therefore are not troubled by them, but it is difficult to see how *Weil* could be satisfied with this response, as she *is* so troubled. If a pedestrian asks me for the time, he is not likely to be puzzled by philosophical questions about the nature of time, and of course it would be absurd for me to embroil him in such questions. But it does not follow from this that those who *are* puzzled by the concept of time would be better off leaving the question alone. As a philosopher, Weil *could not* leave them alone, least of all when they concerned spiritual matters, so she would probably have told Thibon that, if the guardians of the Church professed, and demanded allegiance to, doctrines that could be seen to be spiritually impoverished, unjust, or in other ways problematic, it was her *duty* to question them. It is true that certain kinds of philosophy may get in the way of religious belief, but equally true that philosophy, if practised conscientiously and disinterestedly, can expose superficial modes of worship and thereby help to deepen the faith.

As for the doctrinal elements of the faith, isn't there also a case to be made for saying that the believer *ought* to know them, especially when their denial is branded as heresy, with the threat of excommunication, etc.? What Perrin and Thibon are overlooking is that Weil no more has a *choice* about examining her life, including its religious dimension, through the 'purifying' lens of philosophical analysis than she has about remaining on the threshold of the Church. 'My vocation', she says, 'imposes upon me the necessity of remaining outside the Church ... in order that I may serve God and the Christian faith in the realm of the intelligence.'[42] And why should there not be a vocation, a God-given calling, to adopt a contemplative stance towards matters of the intellect? Hence Weil's insistence that

> [T]he degree of intellectual honesty that is obligatory for me, by reason of my particular vocation, demands that my thought should be indifferent to all ideas without exception, including for instance materialism and atheism; it must be equally welcoming and equally reserved with regard to every one of them.[43]

We should note, incidentally, how similar this conception of philosophical activity is to Wittgenstein's, according to which 'the philosopher is not a citizen of any community of ideas. That is what makes him into a philosopher.'[44] Even so, Weil does not see – and neither does Wittgenstein, for that matter – a contradiction between her philosophical vocation and the love of God.[45] Indeed, would she have been able to penetrate into the core of the Christian faith as deeply as she has, *without* that vocation? If not, then a love of God may well express itself in a reluctance to embrace this or that religious doctrine without critical enquiry, and in the calling to provide an impartial perspective on atheism and belief alike.

But doesn't Weil place rather too much emphasis on *reason*, as Perrin and Thibon have suggested? It is true that, if her criticisms of the Church were motivated by a demand for a rational explanation of everything the believer holds dear, there would be no room for the mystical, unsayable, or ineffable, and she could be charged with propagating a cult of reason. But she is clearly not doing that, so the reasons for her critical attitude towards the Church must be sought elsewhere. The first point to note in this connection is that, contrary to what Weil's earlier remark may have suggested about the relation between St John's conception of faith and the doctrinal articulations of its various dogmas, Weil *does* accord the Church an important role in the preservation of Christ's teaching:

> The function of the Church as the collective keeper of dogma is indispensable. She has the right and the duty to punish those who make a clear attack upon her within the specific range of this function, by depriving them of the sacraments.[46]

As a direct consequence of its spiritual stewardship, the Church must fend off heretical beliefs which pose a serious threat to revealed truth, including the mysteries of the Incarnation and the Eucharist:

> The speculations which it is legitimate to condemn as heretical are those which diminish the reality of divine things by veiling, under the appearance of reconciling them, the contradictions which are their mystery. For example, making the Son an only half-divine being. Or modifying the divinity and the humanity in Christ so as to reconcile them. Or reducing the bread and wine of the Eucharist to a mere symbol. The mysteries then cease to be an object of contemplation; they are no longer of any use.[47]

For Weil, such heresies are the result of an 'illegitimate use of the intelligence' and ought to be condemned, though not necessarily by excluding its perpetrators from the Church.[48] Such a response would be no less excessive and uncharitable than the Church's reaction to the Cathars, a heretical Christian sect which flourished in Western Europe in the twelfth and thirteenth centuries:

> Since the Cathars seem to have carried spiritual freedom to the point of dispensing with all dogmas, a position which is not free from objections, it was quite undoubtedly necessary that the Church should preserve the Christian dogma elsewhere in its integrity, like a diamond, with incorruptible strictness. But a little more faith would have prevented the conclusion that this necessitated their total extermination.[49]

What troubled Weil about the Church's relation to dogma, then, was not so much the dogma as such, as the Church's uncharitable reaction to those who find themselves unable to affirm it. Mindful of the distinction between faith in Christ and intellectual assent to the proposition 'God exists', Weil similarly argues that 'the dogmas of the faith are not things to be affirmed' but 'things to be regarded from a certain distance, with attention, respect and love'.[50] If Weil was reluctant to cross the threshold of the Church, it was probably also because she was afraid that this distance might no longer be granted her, and that she would have felt under an obligation to embrace with her intellect what could only be grasped with faith and love.

Another reason for Weil's refusal to join the Church is her (personal) aversion to anything *collective*. 'My natural disposition', she notes, 'is to be very easily influenced, too much influenced, and above all by anything collective'.[51] To appreciate the force of her remark, one only needs to recall the seductive power of peer pressure, of the tendency of large organisations to accumulate power and to seek ways of perpetuating themselves by stifling opposition and dissent within their own ranks. Vaclav Havel's story, mentioned earlier on, of the 'good' greengrocer who displays his slogans among the carrots and onions in his shop window would be one example here; the oppressive bureaucracy of the Russian Communist party would be another. If Weil is right in thinking that the corrupting influence of power is a *necessary* feature of a collectivity or social structure as such, then the Church as a social structure is just as much prone to this influence as any other collectivity. The root of the problem, however, is a common and natural tendency in all of us. As C. S. Lewis puts it:

> Alone among unsympathetic companions, I hold certain views and standards timidly, half ashamed to avow them, and half doubtful if they can after all be right. Put me back among my friends and in half an hour – in ten minutes – these same views and standards become once more indisputable.[52]

Weil herself gives the following example, prompted by her experiences in Germany:

> I know that if at this moment I had before me a group of twenty young Germans singing Nazi songs in chorus, a part of my soul would instantly become Nazi. That is a very great weakness, but that is how I am.[53]

What Weil is talking about here is, of course, not merely a personal characteristic, but tendencies – to unreason, sentimentality, spontaneous feelings of group solidarity, etc. – to which we are all prone. It would be absurd to interpret her remark as yet another expression of latent anti-Semitism or, worse still, a secret attraction to Nazi ideology.

As for Weil's reluctance to be baptised and so 'officially' received into the Catholic Church, we know that her decision is not the product of intellectual obtuseness, but the consequence of long and serious reflection. She is adamant to the end that '[her] vocation and God's will are opposed to it',[54] and, equally importantly, that she is *unworthy* of this sacrament,[55] as it requires a spiritual depth and purity of soul that she feels is still lacking. Father Perrin may very much have wished her to overcome her reservations, not least because it pained him to know that a part of her fervently longed to participate in the sacraments, but she took them much too seriously for that, and would have considered it dishonest to be baptised just so as to spare Perrin further anxiety.

The miraculous

Before concluding our discussion, we should also say something about Weil's remarks on the miraculous. She addresses the issue because she is not at all convinced that the Church has a clear and consistent position on the matter:

> If the Church does not work out a satisfactory doctrine concerning so-called miraculous facts, a good many souls will be lost through its fault because of the apparent incompatibility between religion and science.[56]

Are miracles incompatible with science? If so, in what way? Does the Church want to insist that miraculous events are clear infringements of the laws of nature, such that there can be *no* natural explanation of such events? And does the scientist insist that, while there may well be extraordinary occurrences, these nevertheless *must* have some naturalistic explanation or other, even if none has been produced thus far? And what is a law of nature, anyway? In Weil's view, the matter requires urgent examination, partly because it seriously distracts believers from what is important in their faith, and partly because the Church is in danger of lapsing into superstition and anti-scientific irrationalism of a kind that will drive many away from its fold. Weil's own view of the miraculous is well captured in the following remark:

> There are several possible ways of conceiving the nature of such acts. There is one which is compatible with the scientific conception of the world. For that reason it is to be preferred. The scientific conception of the world, if properly understood, must not be divorced from true faith. God has created this universe as a network of second causes; it would seem to be impious to suppose there to be holes in this network, as though God were unable to attain his ends save by tampering with his own creative act. If the existence of such holes is admitted, it becomes a scandal that God should not contrive some in order to save the innocent from affliction.[57]

How, then, are we to understand talk of the miraculous in the concreteness of life? Here is an example of which Weil would approve.

At the end of the battle of Agincourt, Shakespeare has Henry V say the following lines:

> O God, thy arm was here!
> And not to us, but to thy arm alone,
> Ascribe we all! When, without stratagem,
> But in plain shock and even play of battle,
> Was ever known so great and little loss
> On one part and on th' other? Take it, God,
> For it is none but thine![58]

Readers of Shakespeare's play will have no difficulty understanding these lines as an expression of religious faith and, given the surrounding circumstances (a battle won against all odds, etc.), as an expression of gratitude, praise, and indeed humility, for what is Henry and his military acumen compared with the majesty and greatness of God? Henry is thankful to God because his victory is a *miracle*. After the siege of Harfleur, his army had suffered greatly, especially from disease, and was quite inadequate for what lay ahead. Most of his 8,000 men, 6,500 of them archers, suffered from dysentery, while the Dauphin had already assembled a powerful force of well over 30,000 men on the other side and, much to Henry's disadvantage, also selected the battlefield. From a military point of view, there was thus hardly a chance of winning the battle, and it is easy to imagine Henry's astonishment when he later learnt that the French casualties outnumbered the entire English force, while of his own men 'only' a few hundred had died; a miracle, indeed. Note how, when Henry addresses his men after the battle, there is no question that his men share the same belief in a gracious and merciful God that also lies at the heart of his own faith:

Henry.	Come, go we in procession to the village;
	And be it death proclaimed through our host
	To boast of this, or take that praise from God
	Which is his only.
Fluellen.	Is it not lawful, an please your Majesty, to tell how
	many is kill'd?
Henry.	Yes, Captain; but with this acknowledgment,
	That God fought for us.
Fluellen.	Yes, my conscience, he did us great good.[59]

But let us take a closer look at what is involved in Henry's belief that his army's victory at Agincourt was a miracle. On the face of it, there are two ways of describing the miraculous nature of the outcome – one in terms of curious metaphysical goings-on, and another in terms of human hopes and expectations, fears and anxieties at the prospect of death and defeat, etc. A description of the first kind might take the following form: when Henry says of God, 'thy arm was here! And not to us, but to thy arm alone, Ascribe we all!', he could be taken to mean that God led him and his army to victory by, in some sense, *causally* interfering in the battle on Henry's behalf, and that it is Henry's belief in this mysterious interference that prompts him to speak of his victory as a miracle.

But if Henry means that, analogously to a human arm, God's 'arm' is to be understood as a genuine, though somewhat unusual, causal agent in the world, then wouldn't his belief be superstitious? Indeed, is there not also something presumptuous in suggesting that he *must* think of the miraculous in such terms? It is telling, for example, that Fluellen does not go on to ask Henry: 'What do you think, my liege, *how* did God do it?' That such questions are not asked by Fluellen (or indeed by the majority of those who witness the miracles in the Scriptures) indicates, not only that they are not considered to be genuine questions in the first place, but that the picture of the miraculous that is at work here may be quite different from the metaphysical picture drawn above.

135

One way of bringing this out is to ask how Henry would react if he were presented with a perfectly natural explanation of why he had won the battle. For example, one might confront Henry with the sort of account now to be found in A. D. Innes's *History of England*, which provides a good explanation of *why* the French forces performed so poorly:

> The English line began to move forward. But the French would no longer be restrained. The cavalry attempted to charge, the French van rolling on behind them. But the archers were prepared with an improvised palisade of pointed stakes. They halted, thrust these into the soft ground, and from behind them began to pour forth their arrows on the advancing masses. The cavalry were rolled over; the heavy armed infantry pressing forward were flung into confusion. The English archers and men-at-arms fell upon them, hewed them down, and hurled themselves upon the second line, which in turn broke and scattered after a brief resistance. The third line was seized with panic...[60]

Now it is tempting to think that, if *this* is the explanation of why Henry won the battle of Agincourt, then there would seem to be no room for the miraculous at all. Given that Henry himself would accept Innes's account of what happened on the battlefield as an account of what happened, surely his insistence that 'God Fought for us' can only mean that he would *not* consider Innes's account as 'the whole story'? And it is only in so far as it is not the whole story that he can see the outcome as miraculous. Or so it might be argued.

However, Henry's acceptance of Innes's account may be quite compatible with seeing his victory as a miracle, precisely because Henry looks for the miraculous in a different place. What is miraculous is that he should have won against all odds, and lost comparatively few soldiers, even though his men were sick and considerably outnumbered by the enemy; that, even though the enemy had selected the battleground (soft ploughland), it turned out to be ideally suited for erecting improvised palisades of the sort that Henry's archers set up. Thus, what would normally have been a great disadvantage (not choosing the battleground) unexpectedly turns out to be distinctly advantageous for Henry's army, and this, too, enters into his description of the outcome as a miraculous one.

It is against the background of such contingencies, of features of the situation which are beyond Henry's (or anyone else's) control, that talk of God's will and utterances like 'And how thou pleasest, God, dispose the day!',[61] become meaningful. Henry's life is not in his own hands at that point, and what would be a better expression of this than to say that his life is in the hands of God? It is because *this* is the way Henry thinks of his life that his subsequent praise of God is only natural and, given his religious orientation, to be expected: God preserved his life and that of his men, and thus he deserves to be praised for it, where it is understood that such praise is not praise for having *done* something that would be independent of whatever Henry and his men did during the battle. To think that praising God is the same as praising a military officer for destroying an ammunition depot of the enemy forces is to forget the way in which religious language enters our lives.

One might object that such a description of the meaning of religious utterances looks no different from what a non-religious man would say in a similar situation, except that the latter would not use religious terminology. Thus, Henry's words have exactly the same meaning as the atheist's 'I hope it goes well' uttered before the battle, and 'That was close, but we *did* it!' after the battle is over. But are they *really* the same? One reason for thinking that they are not is that the relation between Henry's life and the language he uses in talking about it is not an external, but an internal relation. In other words, Henry's life is one whose character could not be revealed except through the very language he uses, just as the character of the atheist's life is revealed in the way *he* talks and thinks about it. By way of illustration, take Henry's prayer shortly before the battle:

O God of battles, steel my soldier's hearts,
Possess them not with fear! Take from them now
The sense of reck'ning, if th' opposed numbers
Pluck their hearts from them. Not to-day, O Lord,
O, not to-day, think not upon the fault
My father made in compassing the crown!
I Richard's body have interred new;
And on it have bestowed more contrite tears
Than from it issued forced drops of blood.
Five hundred poor I have in yearly pay,
Who twice a day their wither'd hands hold up
Toward heaven, to pardon blood; and I have built
Two chantries, where the sad and solemn priests
Sing still for Richard's soul. More will I do!

Though all that I can do is nothing worth,
Since that my penitence comes after all,
Imploring pardon.[62]

In the light of this prayer, Henry's emphatic praise of God after the battle of Agincourt assumes a further dimension, viz. that he can properly see his victory as God having *answered* his earlier prayer. It has been answered because, first, his soldiers were not afraid – 'th' opposed numbers' did not '[p]luck their hearts from them' – and this was something to be thankful for, as there can be no military success without military discipline and the virtues that go with it, such as courage, determination to win, etc. In this connection, it is important to note that Henry's *own* speech, the famous 'Crispin' speech,[63] plays a crucial role in instilling into his men those very virtues, so that it would be quite proper for Henry to see himself as an *instrument* of God in this respect. And in so far as he does that, his own actions constitute an important part of the answer to his prayer.

But the prayer has been answered in a different sense, too. Henry's 'Not to-day, O Lord' must be understood as an allusion to his father Bolingbroke's role in the deposition and murder of Richard II, and thus also to Henry's firm conviction that, because of his father's deed, his own life has been tainted with evil as well, and that he shall be held accountable for it. Even so, he prays to God that he be allowed to survive the battle, not least so that he can engage in further acts of penance. Not surprisingly, therefore, Henry regards his survival as God's answer to his prayer and, indeed, as an expression of God's mercy and forgiveness.

Henry V died in 1422, and hence 66 years before Thomas à Kempis's *Imitation of Christ* was first published. Had he lived to read it, the following passage would no doubt have made a particularly strong impression on him:

Therefore, refer all things to Me, for it is I who have given all to you. Consider everything as Springing from the supreme Good, since to Myself, as their Source, must all things return. ... Therefore, ascribe no good to yourself, nor to any man, but ascribe all to God, without whom man has nothing. I have given all, and it is My will that all return to Me again; I shall require a grateful and exact account. ... If you are truly wise, you will rejoice and hope in Me alone; for none is good but God alone, who is to be praised above all, and to be blessed in all.[64]

I said above that the example of Henry V's miraculous victory at Agincourt exemplifies for Weil a conception of the miraculous that 'is to be preferred' because it is compatible with a scientific account of what happened. This does not mean, however, that Weil would deny the occurrence of miracles that could *not* be explained in naturalistic terms. What she is concerned to preserve, rather, is the idea of a God who works *through* the laws and regularities which govern his creation, rather than as an external cause which arbitrarily interferes with, or suspends, these regularities.

Last things

One of the three questions that, in Immanuel Kant's view, take up the whole of philosophy, is 'What may I hope?' (the other two being 'What can I know?' and 'How ought I to live?'), which concerns God's existence, the immortality of the soul, and life after death. Did Weil hope for the resurrection of the dead and the life of the world to come? Her repeated emphasis on the need for de-creation and self-renunciation already hints at an answer, viz. that she, personally, does not expect to continue to exist beyond the grave. 'As to eventual meetings in another world,' she tells Father Perrin in a letter, 'I do not picture things to myself in that way',[65] and elsewhere she confesses that 'if the Gospel omitted all mention of Christ's resurrection, faith would be easier for me. The Cross by itself suffices me.'[66] It is tempting to take these remarks as a categorical rejection of belief in the resurrection of the dead, but Weil's thoughts on the subject are too few and too varied to amount to a sustained discussion, let alone to an eschatology. The reasons for her cautious attitude are predominantly personal, though she also thinks that the common hope for personal immortality is rooted in a general 'hunger for the temporal' that was 'at first assuaged by the expectation of the imminent Second Coming. Then, when that expectation had worn out, it was assuaged by the Empire. And then, after the sack of Rome, by the Church.'[67] Elsewhere, she insists that the hope for a prolongation of life 'robs death of its purpose',[68] and that, since we should, in any case, 'set aside the beliefs which fill up voids, soften bitternesses', it would be best to abandon the hope for personal immortality as well.[69] Indeed, Weil is clear in her own mind that 'we must completely accept death as annihilation.'[70]

Now, it is true that belief in an afterlife may be the product of denial, of a stubborn reluctance to accept the inevitable, or the result of a self-interested expectation of compensation for all the misfortunes and afflictions endured in this life. Moreover, Weil is certainly right in noting that there are deep and shallow conceptions of death, and that belief in a temporal existence beyond the grave may cheapen the significance of our mortality. On the other hand, if human life is an expression of God's unconditional and unending love, as the Christian tradition affirms it to be, then it is difficult to see why there should be anything superficial, shallow, or egocentric about the hope that God will grant those who love him an existence that extends well beyond their physical demise. After all, if man has been created in God's image, and Christ's teaching is taken to be true, then indifference to the eschatological dimension of his word would be both confused and a sign of ingratitude. Weil may have thought herself unworthy to be resurrected to eternal life in the presence of the Lord, but it does not follow from this that she must also think of her death as complete annihilation. For a true follower of Christ, this would be one thought too many.

Concluding remarks

As we have seen, Weil's contribution to our understanding of the Christian spirit may, indeed, be called outstanding. Her reflections on Christianity, like her thoughts on its intimations among the ancient Greeks and Egyptians, or her critical comments on the Old Testament conception of the divine, are not merely reminders of Christianity's inheritance, or a pious attempt to rescue a legacy we are about to lose. This would make Weil a perceptive commentator on the genealogy of Christian belief, but not the penetrating Christian thinker that she is.

What warrants that description, in the end, is her reminder of what it means to be a Christian as well as a true Catholic. For properly understood, the two are identical. Genuine Catholicism endorses any mode of life that is marked by the spirit of Christ, and one that is universal and inclusive in the way that institutionalized Christianity is not at present. It includes much of what would now be considered 'pagan', and a great deal of what has been, and still is, regarded as 'heretical'. Weil is not blurring the distinction between belief and atheism, however, nor is she claiming that even those who do not pray, go to church, or view their lives under religious descriptions are secretly all believers. Her intention is not to dissolve the general distinctions between belief and unbelief, the religious and the secular, or orthodoxy and heresy, but to shift the boundaries of these terms. This is partly accomplished by loosening the dictates of doctrine, and partly by attentive reflection on what a life in Christ demands of us.

As Weil's own life shows, it does not mean facile ecumenism, or the belief that all religions are basically the same. There are deep and shallow conceptions of God, life, and death, and this distinction still operates as strongly as it did before. Nor does it mean that religious faith is essentially a matter of what the individual makes of it, rejecting all authority and tradition. Weil is well aware that, without its tradition, Christianity would be deprived of its past, of a history of spiritual nourishment and deepened understanding provided by the Church Fathers and religious writers. The Gospels and their interpretation are, of course, the *sine qua non* of this past and, like the other religious traditions Weil speaks about, must be treasured, saved, and transmitted. On the other hand, she is also adamant that it is the concrete life in Christ that matters for our salvation. What the demands of such a life amount to is revealed most forcefully by her reflections on self-effacement, self-renunciation, and emptying of oneself to the point of becoming nothing. Through these reflections, Weil intends to awaken believers to the meaning of their existential predicament, as well as to the task that lies before them.

The picture she draws of the human condition is a sobering one, to be sure: austere in its requirements, and far from the comfortable 'lifestyle' prophets with their pseudo-religious idolatry. The joy derived from the knowledge and trust that our salvation does, indeed, lie in Christ is a joy tempered by the recognition of our fallenness and the uncomfortable acknowledgement that the only path to salvation is through the cross. Like a prophet, Weil breaks through barriers of doctrine, theology, and ideology, to proclaim a faith that is at once more open, as well as more uncompromising, than what many of those who now describe themselves as Christians would be prepared to accept.

Notes

Introduction

1   R. S. Thomas, 'Apostrophe', in R. S. Thomas, *Collected Poems 1945–1990* (London: Phoenix, 2004), 482.

1. Simone Weil's Life

1   Gabriella Fiori, *Simone Weil: An Intellectual Biography* (Athens, Ga: University of Georgia Press, 1989), 15.

2   Ibid., 16.

3   Ibid.

4   Jacques Cabaud, *Simone Weil: A Fellowship in Love* (London: Harvill Press, 1964), 19.

5   Quoted in Simone Pétrement, *Simone Weil: A Life* (New York: Pantheon, 1976), 28.

6   Reprinted in SL, 13.

7   Cabaud, *Simone Weil*, 21.

8   Fiori, *Simone Weil*, 23.

9   Cabaud, *Simone Weil*, 33.

10   Ibid., 28.

11   Ibid., 26.

12   Ibid., 32.

13   'Les Modes d'exploitation', *L'Effort*, 30 Jan. 1932, quoted in Cabaud, *Simone Weil*, 50.

14   J.-M. Perrin and G. Thibon, *Simone Weil As We Knew Her* (London: Routledge, 1953), 124–5.

15   Cabaud, *Simone Weil*, 95.

16   J. P. Little, *Simone Weil* (Oxford: Berg, 1988), 23.

17   Letter to Simone Pétrement, 20 Mar. 1934, quoted in Fiori, *Simone Weil*, 97.

18   WG, 67.

19   Cabaud, *Simone Weil*, 128.

20   WG, 67–8.

21   WG, 69.

22   SL, 158.

23   Quoted in Pétrement, *Simone Weil*, 392.

24   SL, 14.

25   WG, 73.

26   SL, 156.

27   Ibid.

28   Quoted in Pétrement, *Simone Weil*, 479.

29   SL, 201.

2. An Apprenticeship in Attention

1   Weil's spiritual development, her thoughts on the nature and love of God, and her refusal to be baptised will be discussed at greater length in Chapter 5–7.

2   WG, 64 (my emphasis).

3   Fiori, *Simone Weil*, 20.

4   The quotations are from Kleist's well-known letter to Wilhelmine von Zenge, dated 22 Mar. 1801. See Heinrich von Kleist, *Sämtliche Werke und Briefe*, vol. ii (Munich: Carl Hanser, 1977), 633–5, 638. The impact of Kant's œuvre on Kleist comes out particularly clearly in his early play *Die Familie Schroffenstein* (1803), as well as in *Prinz Friedrich von Homburg*, which also bears on the Kantian distinction between duty and inclination.

5   Kleist, *Sämtliche Werke*, ii, 667, quoted in Joseph O. Baker, *The Ethics of Life and Death with Heinrich von Kleist* (Frankfurt: Peter Lang, 1992), 12. The Kantian distinction between the world as a collection of phenomena, and the transcendental basis of these phenomena, will be taken up again in Chapter 3. For a good analytical introduction to Kant's theoretical philosophy, see Georges Dicker, *Kant's Theory of Knowledge* (Oxford: Oxford University Press, 2004), especially 43–8. A reading of Kant that seems to me both plausible and superior to Kleist's interpretation is exemplified in Henry E. Allison, *Kant's Transcendental Idealism* (New Haven, Conn.: Yale University Press, 1983). According to Allison, Kant is not claiming that there are two worlds, one accessible to our experience and another which is not, but *one* world, alternatively conceivable under two different aspects. On this view, it

would be a confusion to think that we can never know what 'reality' is like, as the notion of 'reality' is itself much broader than we might think. I shall return to this issue in Chapter 3.

6   It might be objected that, if the argument in question was not merely speculative and persuasive from a logical point of view, but found to be genuinely convincing, experiences of utter despair and hopelessness would be perfectly intelligible. I am not denying this, of course, but inviting reflection on what it *means* for an argument to be convincing in a way that goes deep, rather than remaining a purely intellectual exercise, and here it seems to me that no argument engenders despair independently of the character of the person who is contemplating it. This issue will be pursued further in Chapter 5, within the context of religious belief. I am greatly indebted to Brian Davies for his valuable comments on this point.

7   Heinrich von Kleist, letter to Adolphine von Werdeck, 19 July 1801, in *Sämtliche Werke und Briefe*, vol. iv (Frankfurt: Deutsches Klassiker Verlag, 1997), 257.

8   Heinrich von Kleist, letter to his sister Ulrike, 5 Feb. 1801, ibid., 197. 117.

9   LOP, 195.

10   SL, 122; cf. Angelica Krogmann, *Simone Weil* (Frankfurt: Rowohlt, 1970), 48–9.

11   Friedrich Nietzsche, letter to his sister Elisabeth, June 1865; quoted in Walter Kaufmann, *Nietzsche*, 4th edn (Princeton, NJ: Princeton University Press, 1974), 23–4.

12   Friedrich Nietzsche, *On the Advantage and Disadvantage of History for Life*, trans. Peter Preuss (Indianapolis: Hackett, 1980), 24.

13   Ibid., 41.

14   Ludwig Wittgenstein, *Tractatus Logico-Philosophicus*, trans. D. F. Pears and B. F. McGuinness (London: Routledge and Kegan Paul, 1969), 6.52, 149.

15   Kleist, *Sämtliche Werke und Briefe*, vol. iv, 117.

16   WG, 66.

17   WG, 64 (my emphasis).

18   WG, 112.

19   WG, 68 (my emphasis).

20   WG, 71 (my emphasis).

21   WG, 105.

22   WG, 115–16.

23   WG, 106–7.

24   WG, 110.

25   WG, 107.

26   WG, 107.

27   WG, 111.

28   WG, 108.

29   WG, 108.

30   For a more detailed discussion of Weil's relation to the latter, see Richard H. Bell, *Simone Weil: The Way of Justice as Compassion* (New York: Rowman and Littlefield, 1998), 147–65.

31   Ibid., 149.

32   Cf. *The New Encyclopaedia Britannica: Macropaedia*, 15th edn, vol. xviii (London: Encyclopaedia Britannica, 1986), 67.

33   WG, 108–9.

34   WG, 111.

35   WG, 111.

36   GG, 107.

37   'What has to be overcome is not a difficulty of the intellect, but of the will': Ludwig Wittgenstein, *Philosophical Occasions*, ed. J. Klagge and A. Nordman (Indianapolis: Hackett, 1993), 161.

38   WG, 112.

39   WG, 105.

40   WG, 105.

41   WG, 106.

42   WG, 108.

43   WG, 106.

44   Thomas Mann, *The Magic Mountain*, trans. H. T. Lowe-Porter (London: Penguin, 1960), 218–19.

45   Ibid., 219.

46   Ibid., 2.

47   Ibid., 296.

48   Ibid., 292.

49   Ibid., 298.

50   WG, 114.

51   Mann, *The Magic Mountain*, 26–7.

52   For a fine discussion of this point, see Raimond Gaita, *Good and Evil* (London: Macmillan, 1991), 304–10.

53   Hannah Arendt, *Eichmann in Jerusalem: A Report on the Banality of Evil* (New York: Viking Press, 1964), 252.

54   Gaita, *Good and Evil*, 306.

55   Arendt, *Eichmann in Jerusalem*, 46.

56   Ibid., 49.

57   Ibid.

58   Ibid., 50–1.

59   Ibid., 51.

60   WG, 115.

61   NB, i, 103.

62   Arendt, *Eichmann in Jerusalem*, 252.

63   NB, ii, 492.

64   D. Z. Phillips, 'Dislocating the Soul', in D. Z. Phillips (ed.), *Can Religion Be Explained Away?* (London: Macmillan, 1996), 247.

3. A Philosophical Apprenticeship

1   Oliver Sacks, *Uncle Tungsten* (London: Picador, 2001), 26.

2   Ibid.

3   Ibid.

4   IC, 164.

5   SL, 116.

6   SL, 117–18.

7   SL, 117.

8   SL, 125.

9   WG, 63.

10   IC, 189.

11   IC, 151.

12   IC, 185.

13   LP, 24.

14   David McLellan, *Simone Weil: Utopian Pessimist* (London: Macmillan, 1989), 205.

15   Rush Rhees, *Discussions of Simone Weil* (Albany, NY: State University of New York Press, 1999), 64.

16   SL, 131.

17   IC, 153.

18   IC, 171.

19   SL, 131.

20   SL, 118.

21   IC, 171.

22   IC, 172.

23   IC, 164–5.

24   SL, 115.

25   IC, 152.

26   See Andre Maurois's preface to Alain, *Propos*, vol. i (Paris: Gallimard, 1956), p. vii.

27   See Richard Pevear's introduction to Alain, *The Gods* (London: Chatto and Windus, 1975), 6.

28   Ibid.

29   SWR, 288.

30   SWR, 271.

31   SWR, 288.

32   SWR, 294.

33   SN, 162.

34   OC VI.1, 174.

35   FW, 284.

36   Alain, *The Gods*, 92.

37   Plato, *Republic*, 514a, trans. G. M. A. Grube, revd C. D. C. Reeves (Indianapolis: Hackett, 1997).

38   Ibid., 514c.

39   Ibid.

40   SN, 106.

41   SN, 109.

42   SN, 108–9.

43   SN, 109.

44   Immanuel Kant, *Critique of Pure Reason*, B311, trans. Norman Kemp Smith (London: Macmillan, 1986).

45   Immanuel Kant, 'Reflexionen zur Metaphysik', no. 4135, in Preussische Akademie der Wissenschaften (eds), *Kants Gesammelte Schriften* (Berlin: de Gruyter, 1926), xvii, 429.

46   Ibid., no. 6057, in *Kants Gesammelte Schriften*, xviii, 440.

47   For a good discussion of this issue, see Karl-Heinz Michel, *Immanuel Kant und die Frage der Erkennbarkeit Gottes* (Wuppertal: R. Brockhaus, 1987).

48   LOP, 220.

49   LOP, 221.

50   LOP, 147.

51   LOP, 147.

52   Quoted in Cabaud, *Simone Weil*, 54.

53   GG, 114.

54   André Maurois, *Mémoires*, vol. i (Paris: Flammarion, 1948), 53; cf. Pétrement, *Simone Weil*, 34.

55   OC I, 67 (trans. Martin Andic).

56   OC I, 68.

57   OC I, 68.

58   OC I, 69.

59   OC I, 71.

4. Politics and the Needs of the Soul: Factory Work

1   OL, 22.

2   SL, 15.

3   Reprinted in FW, 149–226.

4   Included in SWR, 53–72.

5   SWR, 54.

6   NR, 16.

7   NR, 34.

8   NR, 34.

9   NR, 35.

10   NR, 45.

11   OL, 45.

12   SWR, 54.

13   SWR, 54.

14   SWR, 55.

15   SWR, 55.

16   SWR, 56.

17   SWR, 56.

18   SWR, 56.

19   SWR, 57.

20   SWR, 57.

21   OL, 76.

22   SWR, 57.

23   NR, 297.

24   SWR, 57.

25   SWR, 58–9.

26   NR, 36.

27   Vaclav Havel, 'The Power of the Powerless', in Vaclav Havel, *Living in Truth* (London: Faber and Faber, 1986), 36–122.

28   See the section entitled 'Truth', in NR, 36–9.

29   Havel, 'The Power of the Powerless', 41.

30   Ibid.

31   Ibid., 42.

32   Ibid., 45.

33   SWR, 59.

34   SWR, 60.

35   SWR, 61.

36   OL, 16; see also OL, 13.

37   SWR, 63.

38   OL, 78.

39   SWR, 66.

40   SWR, 67.

41   SWR, 68.

42   SWR, 71.

43   SWR, 71.

44   SWR, 61.

45   See Ray Monk, *Bertrand Russell: The Spirit of Solitude* (London: Vintage, 1996), 26.

46   Mann, *The Magic Mountain*, 245–6.

47   OL, 154.

5. Religious Reflection (1): God, the Christian Inspiration, and the Incarnation

1   'Thoughts without content are empty, intuitions without concepts are blind'. Immanuel Kant, *Critique of Pure Reason*, A52/B76. Kant's point is that, if the

mind is to have anything to think *about*, it needs sense experience to do so. Conversely, raw sensations are 'blind', mean nothing, so long as they aren't subsumed under intelligible concepts. The first part of Kant's dictum could also be said to capture Weil's contention that, when thought is not rendered concrete by practical experience, it easily becomes an abstraction.

2   Just as buildings, for example, must conform to general principles of architecture and statics if they are to remain standing, so the 'formal conditions' of an authentic life are the general framework requirements it must satisfy in order to form a unity, e.g. meaning what one says, doing what one intends, etc.

3   GG, p. xxxii.

4   GG, p. xxxii.

5   GG, p. xxxii.

6   WG, 62.

7   Pierre Bertaux, *Friedrich Hölderlin* (Frankfurt: Suhrkamp, 1981).

8   Ludwig Wittgenstein, *Zettel*, 2nd edn, ed. G. E. M. Anscombe and G. H. von Wright (Oxford: Blackwell, 1981), §717.

9   Armin Kreiner, 'What do we mean by "God"?', *New Blackfriars*, no. 1007 (Jan. 2006), 26.

10   Ibid.

11   Rush Rhees, *On Religion and Philosophy*, ed. D. Z. Phillips, assisted by Mario von der Ruhr (Cambridge: Cambridge University Press, 1997), 36.

12   GG, 109–10.

13   For a good discussion of this issue, see Brian Davies, 'The Doctrine of God', in Michael J. Walsh (ed.), *Commentary on the Catechism of the Catholic Church* (London: Geo Chapman, 1994), 50–65.

14   Ibid., 60.

15   NB, i, 243.

16   Isaiah 45.15; cf. Weil's remarks on this verse in NB, i, 149.

17   R. S. Thomas, 'The Absence', in Thomas, *Collected Poems 1945–1990*, 361.

18   NB, i, 424.

19   NB, i, 25.

20   Ludwig Wittgenstein, *Culture and Value*, trans. Peter Winch, 2nd edn (Oxford: Blackwell, 1998), 97.

21   GG, 46.

22   SWW, 85.

23   GG, 13.

24   SWW, 85.

25   WG, 62.

26   WG, 62.

27   WG, 65.

28   WG, 65.

29   WG, 65.

30   WG, 66.

31   FLN, 114.

32   Karl Rahner, *Theological Investigations*, vol. vi, trans. David Bourke (London: Darton, Longman and Todd, 1969), 391.

33   Karl Rahner, *Theological Investigations*, vol. xvi, trans. David Bourke (London: Darton, Longman and Todd, 1976), 283.

34   WG, 62.

35   WG, 71.

36   WG, 70. Emma Craufurd's English translation incorrectly renders 'une incarnation de Dieu' as 'the Incarnation of God'.

37   LP, 22.

38   LP, 22.

39   I am indebted to H. O. Mounce for emphasising the importance of this point.

40   Martin Buber, *Eclipse of God* (New York: Harper and Row, 1957), 28.

41   Ibid., 29.

42   Ibid.

43   Ibid.

44   Ibid.

45   Ibid.

46   Ibid., 30.

47   C. S. Lewis, *Miracles* (London: HarperCollins, 2002), 278–9.

48   Ibid.

49   Gustave Thibon's edition of *Gravity and Grace* has not been included in this list, as it is merely a collection of remarks taken from the *Notebooks*.

50   WG, 55.

51   FLN, 341.

52   FLN, 83; see also GG, 150.

53   FLN, 83.

54   WG, 168.

55   Notes on lectures given by Simone Weil at Le Puy in 1931/2, her first year of

teaching; edited by Gilbert Kahn from the notebooks of Elisabeth Bigot-Chanel and Yvette Argaud, and published in *Cahiers Simone Weil* 8 (1985), 121–6. Translation from an unpublished manuscript by Martin Andic.

56   Ibid.

57   SN, 15.

58   IC, 89.

59   FLN, 50.

60   'Monteverdi, Bach, Mozart were beings whose lives were pure even as were their works': NR, 233.

61   'The Responsibility of Writers', *Cahiers du Sud*, no. 310 (1951). The paper was probably written in the summer of 1941. Reprinted in SN, 167; see also FLN, 29.

62   Roger Scruton, *An Intelligent Person's Guide to Modern Culture* (South Bend, Ind.: St. Augustine's Press, 2000), 106.

63   Ibid., 107.

64   NB, ii, 440.

65   GG, 151.

6. Religious Reflection (2): Christ, Krishna, and the Old Testament

1   GG, 174.

2   *Catechism of the Catholic Church* (New York: Doubleday, 1997), §§464, 130.

3   Ibid., §§480, 135.

4   Immanuel Kant, *The Contest of the Faculties*, in Immanuel Kant, *Religion and Rational Theology*, trans. and ed. Allen W. Wood and George Di Giovanni (Cambridge: Cambridge University Press, 1996), 20.

5   FLN, 130.

6   NB, ii, 379.

7   IC, 168.

8   NB, ii, 576.

9   LP, 14.

10   Plato, *Republic* 472b–473b.

11   Ibid., 472b.

12   NB, ii, 384.

13   IC, 141 (my emphasis).

14   IC, 141.

15   IC, 141.

16 IC, 141–2.

17 IC, 142.

18 *Catechism of the Catholic Church*, §462.

19 NB, ii, 565.

20 NB, ii, 566; see also LP, 8.

21 Hebrews 7.2–4; see also Genesis 14.18–24 and Psalm 110.

22 NB, ii, 566.

23 LP, 8.

24 LP, 4.

25 NB, ii, 561.

26 Perrin and Thibon, *Simone Weil As We Knew Her*, 68.

27 J. Assmann, *Der König als Sonnenpriester* (Cairo: Deutsches Archäologisches Institut, 1970), 22; quoted in Eugen Drewermann, *Discovering the God Child Within*, trans. Peter Heinegg (New York: Crossroads, 1994), 63.

28 Ibid., 73–4.

29 LP, 15.

30 LP, 11.

31 LP, 4.

32 WG, 70.

33 SL, 188.

34 SL, 181.

35 SL, 184.

36 FLN, 322, 336.

37 NB, i, 54, 90, 93, 97, 101, 200, 286, 290, 305, 324; NB, ii, 351, 421–2, 526, 542, 561.

38 SL, 17, 181, 184, 188, 190.

39 *The Bhagavad Gita*, trans. Juan Mascaró (Harmondsworth: Penguin, 1962), 11.54, p. 95.

40 Ibid., 12.18, p. 97.

41 Ibid., 4.6, p. 61.

42 Ibid., 8.5, p. 77.

43 Ibid., 8.22, p. 79.

44 Ibid., 9.18, p. 81.

45 I am indebted to Tim Ketcher for his helpful comments on this issue.

46 *Bhagavad Gita*, 9.23, p. 82.

47 Quoted in *The Christian Faith*, ed. J. Neuner and J. Dupuis, 5th edn (London: HarperCollins, 1991), art. 1018, p. 313.

48 Ibid., art. 804, p. 234.

49 NB, ii, 542.

50 NB, ii, 542.

51 *Bhagavad Gita*, 1.34, 35, 38, 39, p. 46.

52 IC, 39.

53 IC, 39.

54 IC, 54.

55 NB, i, 104–5.

56 SL, 160.

57 NB, i, 104–5.

58 *Bhagavad Gita*, 16.2–3, p. 109

59 SL, 129.

60 LP, 41.

61 LP, 41.

62 SL, 129–30.

63 NB, ii, 570.

64 Gareth Moore, 'Hearing the Voice of God: Two Conceptual Issues Concerning the Relationship Between the Biblical World and Ours', in D. Z. Phillips and Mario von der Ruhr (eds), *Biblical Concepts and Our World* (London: Palgrave, 2004), 23–4.

65 John Barton, *What is the Bible?* (London: SPCK, 1991), 104–5.

66 Ibid.

67 Moore, 'Hearing the Voice of God', 23–4.

68 Perrin and Thibon, *Simone Weil As We Knew Her*, 60.

69 *Bhagavad Gita*, 2.31, 38, p. 51.

70 Ibid., 'Introduction' by Juan Mascaró, p. 23.

71 Ibid., 3.43, p. 60.

72 Ibid., 4.42, p. 65.

73 John 18.36.

74 NB, ii, 542.

75 J. P. Little, *Simone Weil* (Oxford: Berg, 1988), 145.

76 Perrin and Thibon, *Simone Weil As We Knew Her*, 105.

77 NB, i, 145.

78   NB, i, 221.

79   NB, i, 229.

80   LP, 30.

81   Luke 23.41, 42.

82   NB, i, 247.

83   NB, i, 194.

84   Luke 22.33.

85   FLN, 295.

86   NB, ii, 470.

87   D. Z. Phillips, 'Saying Scripture', in D. Z. Phillips, *Religion and Friendly Fire* (Aldershot: Ashgate, 2004), 110.

88   LP, 3.

89   SL, 25.

90   WG, 39.

91   WG, 70.

92   WG, 79.

93   SL, 123.

94   WG, 69.

95   See Teresa of Avila's *The Way of Perfection*, *The Interior Castle*, *Spiritual Relations*, *Exclamations of the Soul to God*, and *Conceptions on the Love of God*; and St John of the Cross's spiritual poems *The Spiritual Canticle*, *The Dark Night of the Soul*, and *The Living Flame of Love*.

96   SL, 139.

7. Religious Reflection (3): Creation, Affliction and Last Things

1   SWW, 79.

2   SWW, 79.

3   NB, i, 480.

4   NB, i, 497.

5   SL, 153.

6   GG, 33.

7   SWW, 72.

8   GG, 32.

9   SWW, 72–3.

10 NB, ii, 423.

11 WG, 75.

12 WG, 88.

13 WG, 75.

14 R. S. Thomas, 'The Island', in Thomas, *Collected Poems 1945–1990*, 223.

15 SWW, 80.

16 SWW, 80.

17 SWW, 80.

18 SWW, 73.

19 SWW, 73.

20 FLN, 136.

21 FLN, 136.

22 WG, 129.

23 WG, 129.

24 WG, 128.

25 WG, 128.

26 SWW, 73.

27 For example, in the new Routledge edition, which also includes an English translation of Gustave Thibon's 1990 postscript to the French edition. For similar comments on Israel, see LP, 1, 4–5, 8–9, 16, 26, 40, 44–5, 48–9, 54–6.

28 GG, 160.

29 GG, 161.

30 GG, 159.

31 Wladimir Rabi, 'La Conception weilienne de la création', in Gilbert Kahn (ed.), *Simone Weil: Philosophe, historienne et mystique* (Paris: Aubier Montaigne, 1978), 141, quoted in Thomas R. Nevin, *Simone Weil* (Chapel Hill, NC: University of North Carolina Press, 1991), 253.

32 Arnold Mandel, 'Repliques à Oscar Wolfman', *Le Monde*, 19 July 1978, p. 2; quoted in Nevin, *Simone Weil*, 256.

33 Perrin and Thibon, *Simone Weil As We Knew Her*, 119.

34 GG, 159.

35 GG, 159.

36 D. Z. Phillips, *The Problem of Evil and the Problem of God* (London: SCM Press, 2004), 231.

37 SL, 155.

38 Perrin and Thibon, *Simone Weil As We Knew Her*, 41.

39   Ibid., 43.

40   Ibid., 156–7.

41   Ibid., 157.

42   WG, 85.

43   WG, 85.

44   Wittgenstein, *Zettel*, §455.

45   WG, 86.

46   WG, 80.

47   FLN, 132–3.

48   FLN, 133.

49   SE, 52.

50   LP, 30.

51   LP, 53.

52   C. S. Lewis, *The Four Loves* (Glasgow: Collins, 1985), 74.

53   WG, 53.

54   WG, 46.

55   WG, 46.

56   LP, 35.

57   LP, 32.

58   Shakespeare, *Henry V*, IV, viii, 100–06.

59   Ibid., IV, viii, 108–15.

60   A. D. Innes, *A History of England* (New York: G. P. Putnam's Sons, 1912), 196.

61   Shakespeare, *Henry V*, IV, iv, 132.

62   Ibid., IV, i, 276–92.

63   Ibid., IV, iii, 40–67.

64   Thomas à Kempis, *The Imitation of Christ*, trans. Leo Sherley-Price (London: Penguin, 1954), 105.

65   WG, 59.

66   LP, 55.

67   FLN, 216.

68   GG, 37.

69   NB, i, 149.

70   NB, ii, 492.

Bibliography

A. Primary texts by Simone Weil

1. English

First and Last Notebooks, trans. and ed. Richard Rees (New York: Oxford University Press, 1970).

Formative Writings 1929–1941, trans. and ed. Dorothy Tuck McFarland and Wilhelmina van Ness (Amherst, Mass.: University of Massachusetts Press, 1987).

Gravity and Grace, trans. Emma Craufurd and Mario von der Ruhr (London: Routledge, 2002); 1st publ. 1947 as *La Pesanteur et la grâce* by Librairie Plon.

Intimations of Christianity among the Ancient Greeks (London: Routledge, 1988); consists of chapters from *La Source grecque*, 1st publ. 1952 by Librairie Gallimard and *Les Intuitions préchrétiennes*, 1st publ. 1951 by Les Éditions de la Colombe.

Lectures on Philosophy, trans. Hugh Price (Cambridge: Cambridge University Press, 1978); 1st publ. 1959 as *Leçons de philosophie* by Librairie Plon.

Letter to a Priest, trans. A. F. Wills (London: Routledge, 2002).

The Need for Roots, trans. A. F. Wills (London: Routledge, 2002); 1st publ. 1949 as *L'Enracinement* by Gallimard.

Notebooks, 2 vols, trans. Arthur Wills (London: Routledge and Kegan Paul, 1956); 1st publ. 1952–5 as *Les Cahiers de Simone Weil*, 3 vols, by Librairie Plon.

On Science, Necessity, and the Love of God, trans. and ed. Richard Rees (London: Oxford University Press, 1968).

Oppression and Liberty, trans. Arthur Wills and John Petrie (London: Routledge, 2001).

Selected Essays, ed. and trans. Richard Rees (London: Oxford University Press, 1962).

Seventy Letters, ed. and trans. Richard Rees (New York: Oxford University Press, 1965).

Simone Weil on Colonialism, trans. and ed. Patricia Little (New York: Rowman and Littlefield, 2003).

Waiting for God, trans. Emma Craufurd (New York: Harper and Row, 1973).

2. French

Cahiers (1933–septembre 1941), ed. André A. Devaux and Florence de Lussy (Paris: Gallimard, 1994); vol. VI.1 of *Œuvres complètes*.

Cahiers (septembre 1941–février 1942), ed. André A. Devaux and Florence de Lussy (Paris: Gallimard, 1997); vol. VI.2 of *Œuvres complètes*.

Cahiers (février 1942–juin 1942), ed. André A.Devaux and Florence de Lussy (Paris: Gallimard, 2002); vol. VI.3 of *Œuvres complètes*.

La Condition ouvrière (Paris: Gallimard, 1951).

La Connaissance surnaturelle (Paris: Gallimard, 1950).

Écrits de Londres et dernières lettres (Paris: Gallimard, 1957).

Écrits historiques et politiques. L'Engagement syndical (1927–juillet 1934), ed. André A. Devaux and Florence de Lussy (Paris: Gallimard, 1988); vol. II.1 of *Œuvres complètes*.

Écrits historiques et politiques. L'Expérience ouvrière et l'adieu à la révolution (juillet 1934–juin 1937), ed. André A. Devaux and Florence de Lussy (Paris: Gallimard, 1991); vol. II.2 of *Œuvres complètes*.

Écrits historiques et politiques. Vers la guerre (1937–1940), ed. André A. Devaux and Florence de Lussy (Paris: Gallimard, 1989); vol. II.3 of *Œuvres complètes*.

L'Enracinement (Paris: Gallimard, 1949).

Leçons de philosophie de Simone Weil (Roanne, 1933–1934), presented by A. Reynaud (Paris: Plon, 1959).

Œuvres complètes, ed. André A. Devaux and Florence de Lussy (Paris: Gallimard, 1988–).

Oppression et Liberté (Paris: Gallimard, 1955).

Pensées sans ordre concernant l'amour de Dieu (Paris: Gallimard, 1962).

Poèmes, suivis de Venise sauvée (Paris: Gallimard, 1968).

Premiers écrits philosophiques, ed. André A. Devaux and Florence de Lussy (Paris: Gallimard, 1988), vol. I of *Œuvres complètes*

Simone Weil. Sa vie – Son enseignement, ed. Julien Molard (Sury-en-Vaux: A à Z Patrimoine, 2004).

B. Useful anthologies of Weil's writings in English

Simone Weil Reader, ed. George A. Panichas (Wakefield, R I and London: Moyer Bell, 1977).
Simone Weil: Writings, selected with an introduction by Eric O. Springsted (Maryknoll, NY: Orbis Books, 1998).

C. Bibliographies

J. P. Little, *Simone Weil: A Bibliography* (London: Grant and Cutler, 1973).
Simone Weil: A Bibliography, Supplement No. 1 (London: Grant and Cutler, 1979).

D. General studies and introductions to Weil

Heinz Abosch, *Simone Weil*, trans. Kimberly A. Kenny (New York: Pennbridge, 1994).
Richard H. Bell, *Simone Weil: The Way of Justice as Compassion* (Lauham, Md: Rowman and Littlefield, 1998).
(ed.), *Simone Weil's Philosophy of Culture* (Cambridge: Cambridge University Press, 1993).
Lawrence A. Blum and Victor J. Seidler, *A Truer Liberty: Simone Weil and Marxism* (London: Routledge, 1989).
Sylvie Courtine-Denamy, *Three Women in Dark Times: Edith Stein, Hannah Arendt, Simone Weil* (Ithaca, NY: Cornell University Press, 2000).
Marie-Madeleine Davy, *The Mysticism of Simone Weil*, trans. Cynthia Rowland (London: Rockliff, 1951).
E. Jane Doering and Eric O. Springsted, *The Christian Platonism of Simone Weil* (Notre Dame, Ind.: University of Notre Dame Press, 2004).
Henry Leroy Finch, *Simone Weil and the Intellect of Grace* (New York: Continuum, 1999).
Christopher Frost and Rebecca Bell-Metereau, *Simone Weil on Politics, Religion and Society* (London: Sage, 1998).
David McLellan, *Simone Weil, Utopian Pessimist* (London: Macmillan, 1989).
J. P. Little, *Simone Weil* (Oxford: Berg, 1988).

Athanasios Moulakis, *Simone Weil and the Politics of Self-Denial*, trans. Ruth Hein (Columbia, Mo.: University of Missouri Press, 1998).

Rush Rhees, *Discussions of Simone Weil*, ed. D. Z. Phillips (Albany, NY: State University of New York Press, 1999).

Peter Winch, *Simone Weil: 'The Just Balance'* (Cambridge: Cambridge University Press, 1989).

E. Material for studying the life of Weil

Jacques Cabaud, *Simone Weil: A Fellowship in Love* (London: Harvill Press, 1964); developed from *L'Expérience vécue de Simone Weil* (Paris: Librairie Plon, 1957).

Gabrielle Fiori, *Simone Weil: An Intellectual Biography*, trans. Joseph R. Berrigan (Athens, Ga and London: University of Georgia Press, 1989).

Francine du Plessix Gray, *Simone Weil* (London: Weidenfeld and Nicolson, 2001).

J.-M. Perrin and G. Thibon, *Simone Weil As We Knew Her* (London: Routledge, 1953, repr. 2003).

Simone Pétrement, *Simone Weil: A Life*, trans. Raymond Rosenthal (London and Oxford: Mowbray, 1976).

Richard Rees, *Simone Weil: A Sketch for a Portrait* (London: Oxford University Press, 1966).

E. W. F. Tomlin, *Simone Weil* (Cambridge: Bowes and Bowes, 1954).

F. Other relevant reading

Alain, *The Gods* (New York: New Directions, 1974).

Raimond Gaita, *A Common Humanity* (London: Routledge, 1998).

Good and Evil: An Absolute Conception (London: Macmillan, 1991).

Vaclav Havel, 'The Power of the Powerless', in Vaclav Havel, *Living in Truth* (London: Faber and Faber, 1986), 36–122.

R. F. Holland, *Against Empiricism* (Totowa, NJ: Barnes and Noble Books, 1980).

C. S. Lewis, *Miracles* (London: HarperCollins, 2002).

D. Z. Phillips, *The Problem of Evil and the Problem of God* (London: SCM Press, 2004).

Religion and Friendly Fire (Aldershot: Ashgate, 2004).

Plato, *Complete Works*, ed. John M. Cooper (Indianapolis and

Cambridge: Hackett, 1997), especially the *Timaeus*, *Phaedrus*, *Symposium*, and *Republic*.

Rush Rhees, *On Religion and Philosophy*, ed. D. Z. Phillips (Cambridge: Cambridge University Press, 1997).

Without Answers (London: Routledge and Kegan Paul, 1969).

Roger Scruton, *An Intelligent Person's Guide to Modern Culture* (South Bend, Ind.: St. Augustine's Press, 2000).

R. S. Thomas, *Collected Poems 1945–1990* (London: Phoenix, 2004).

Explanatory Notes on the Publication of Weil's Work

Essays

The essay 'God in Plato' appears in both *On Science, Necessity and the Love of God* and *Intimations of Christianity among the Ancient Greeks*. The paper 'The Love of God and Affliction' is included in both *On Science, Necessity and the Love of God* and *Waiting for God*.

First and Last Notebooks

The *First Notebook* covers the period 1933–39 and was composed in France; the *Last Notebook* extends from 1942 to 1943 and was written in New York and London. The *Last Notebook* is, in effect, identical with *La Connaissance surnaturelle*, which also contains the 'Prologue' concerning Weil's mystical experience.

Gravity and Grace

This is a selection from her notebooks published in 1947 by Gustave Thibon.

Notebooks

These cover the years 1940 to 1942 (before Marseilles), and include nearly a dozen individual notebooks. The *Cahiers* were originally published by Plon in 1951 (vol. 1), 1953 (vol. 2), and 1955 (vol. 3).

The English translation came out in 1956. A revised and enlarged edition was released by Plon in 1970 (vol. 1), 1972 (vol. 2), and 1974 (vol. 3), and first published in Britain in 1956. In 2004, Routledge released a one-volume edition of the *Notebooks*, which is a reprint of Arthur Wills's 1956 translation of the first French edition (1952–55). Of the projected four-volume Gallimard edition of the *Cahiers*, three have been published thus far. They extend from September 1933 to June 1942, and appeared in 1994 (vol. 1, 1933–September 1941), 1997 (vol. 2, September 1941–February 1942), and 2002 (vol. 3, February 1942–June 1942), respectively,

Collection Espoir

This series, launched in 1946, was founded by Albert Camus and resulted in 24 works. One of these, *L'Embarras du choix* (1947), was written by Brice Parain, who also drew Camus' attention to Simone Weil. From 1949 onwards, Camus began to publish Weil's work, with the following titles appearing in the series:

1. The Need for Roots
2. La Connaissance surnaturelle
3. Lettre à un réligieux
4. La Condition ouvrière
5. La Source grecque
6. Écrits de Londres; Dernières lettres
7. Écrits historiques et politiques
8. Pensées sans ordre concernant l'amour de Dieu
9. Poèmes

Index